Pine Barrens Legends & Lore

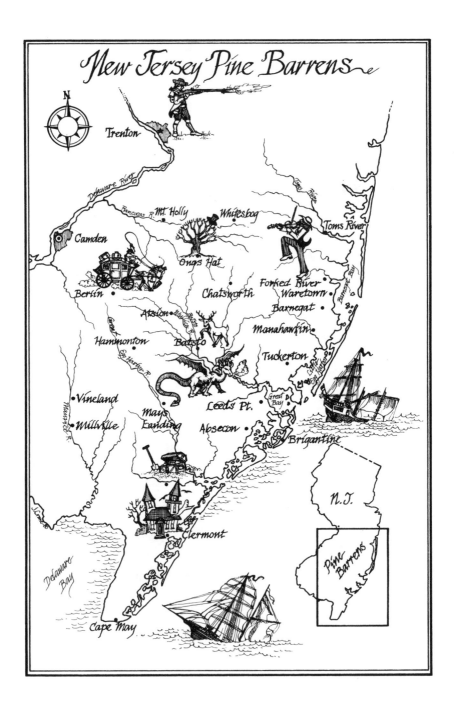

PINE BARRENS LEGENDS & LORE

by William McMahon

MIDDLE ATLANTIC PRESS
Moorestown, New Jersey

Manufactured in the United States of America

3 4 5 02 01 00 99

Library of Congress Cataloging-in-Publication Data
McMahon, William H,
    Pine Barrens legends and lore.

Bibliography: p.139
Includes index.
SUMMARY: Presents legends and lore of the New Jersey Pine Barrens, an area occupying roughly one million acres.
  1. Legends—New Jersey—Pine Barrens. 2. Folklore—New Jersey—Pine Barrens. 3. Pine Barrens—Social life and customs. {1. Folklore—New Jersey—Pine Barrens. 2. Pine Barrens—Social life and customs} I. Title.
GR110.N5M33   398.2'09749'9   80-23518
ISBN 0-912608-19-6

Cover Design and Illustrations: Desireé Keane
with assistance from Brian Rappa

For information write:
Middle Atlantic Press
10 Twosome Drive
P.O. Box 600
Moorestown, NJ 08057

To Betty, who has long awaited this book

Contents

TODAY'S BARRENS

BIBLIOGRAPHY

INDEX

Lovely People

One of the delights in writing this book has been the many interesting people I have met along the road who helped, each in his or her own individual way, with recollections, photographs, and sometimes historical digging.

Some went to great lengths to secure for me the material I asked for or to point out some hidden, winding path or unusual tale I had not before known.

Although Herbert N. Halpert's unpublished doctoral dissertation is listed in the bibliography at the back of this book, I want to acknowledge here my debt to this path-breaking scholarly study of Pinelands folk tales and legends.

My special thanks to William C. Wright, Head, New Jersey Library Bureau of Archives and History and David C. Munn, the bureau's Historical Editor; Joan C. Hull, Executive Director, New Jersey Historical Society and Barbara S. Irwin, the society's Library Director; Philip Alami, Secretary of Agriculture, State of New Jersey; Mrs. Pauline Miller, Ocean County Historian; Annie Carter and James Rozmus, of Batsto; Mrs. Kurt Hoelle, Librarian, Gloucester County Historical Society; Lowry Welch, Historian, Burlington County Historical Society; William Bolger, Historian, Burlington County Cultural and Heritage Commission; Raymond Frankle, Director of Library Services, Stockton State College; William J. Guilfoile, Director of Public Relations, National Baseball Hall of Fame; Ted Gordon; Adrian Phillips; Dr. V. Eugene Vivian, founder of the Environmental Studies Center, Whitesbog; Willard Mason Rogers; Merce Ridgway, Jr.; Herbert Colcord, Ocean Spray Cranberries, Inc.; George Abbott; Janice Sherwood; and Karen Waldauer, the very patient publisher of The Middle Atlantic Press, for help, advice, and putting up with bum typing.

William McMahon

Pine Barrens Legends & Lore

Ruins in the Pines at Weymouth, once a paper mill.

Introduction

I consider myself a Piney by adoption.

Brought up on the edge of the Pines in Gloucester County, I have always been fascinated by this vast region of forests, swamps and streams covering one-fourth of the entire state of New Jersey.

It is a region of mysterious sand hills, restless pines and cedars, ruins of forgotten settlements, exotic flowers and ferns, various wee creatures, winding streams of matchless beauty and cold, pure water—the last great wilderness between New England and the Virginias.

It is a place of romance, legends, adventure and history. Across its great green canvas flash pirates and plunder, patriots and villains, boom towns and ghost towns, historic inns and taverns, brawling railroaders and stagecoach drivers, and dreams—some realized, others forever lost in the dust of time.

The Barrens today occupies roughly one million acres of Ocean, Burlington, Cape May, Cumberland, Camden and Atlantic Counties, with some stretching into Monmouth and Gloucester counties.

It contains the vast Wharton State Forest tract, the Lebanon State Forest, Bass River State Forest, Penn State Forest, Green Bank State Forest, Belleplain State Forest, Parvin State Forest, Corson's Inlet State Park, Fort Mott State Park, Cape Point State Forest, the Brigantine Wild-life Sanctuary, Colliers Mills Fish and Game Preserve, Swan Bay Fish and Wildlife Area, Pasadena Wildlife Area and the Port Republic Wildlife Area.

The Pines also embrace the Batsto and Atsion iron town restorations, the Carranza Memorial to a good-will flight that ended in disaster, the Chestnut Neck battlegrounds of the Revolutionary War, and long forgotten towns such as Hermann City, Crowleytown, Gloucester Furnace,

Part of the elaborate iron ornamentation of the old mill
house at Pleasant Mills. The photo was taken before the
place was abandoned and stripped by vandals.

Harrisville, Catawba, Amatol, Bulltown, Quaker Bridge, Washington, Mathistown, Penny Pot, Whitesbog, Hampton Furnace, Mount Washington, Friendship, Calico, Martha, Pestletown, Butler Place, Four Mile, Upper Mill, Ongs Hat, Union Clay Works, Howardsville, Boar Stag, Cedar Grove, Bard's Neck, Bellowstown, Belly Bridge, and Old Half Way.

The gigantic watershed of the Pinelands is fed by two principal rivers, the Mullica and the Great Egg Harbor, along with such tributaries as the Wading, Oswego, Bass and Tuckahoe rivers. Numerous lakes and small streams, mostly called runs, dot the area.

The Pines were the site of New Jersey's earliest industries: bog iron, glass and paper making. They were once the hideouts of bandit bands such as the Mulliners and the Gibersons. Here circuit riders brought the Bible to lonely settlers, and the Lenni Lenape made their last stand against the invading white man. Here such poets as Walt Whitman found lyric inspiration, botanists made important discoveries, and would-be empire builders created iron and glass towns. Here also is the birthplace of today's giant cranberry and blueberry industries.

The people who inhabited the Pines in the deep past, and whose descendants still do, are known as "Pineys" and have many times been linked to the Kentucky mountain folk—an untrue picture. The origins of the first Pineys are shrouded in mystery, since few family records were kept. One Pines lady told me that although her roots are in the Pinelands the only records she had were verbal, handed down from one generation to another, plus a few notations in a family Bible. Another proudly stated that there was Indian blood in the family line, but her ancesters did not consider it in the same light she does and consequently did everything possible to hide it.

It is known that some of the earliest inhabitants of the Pines were Hessian mercenaries who deserted after the battle of Trenton in the American Revolution and lost themselves in the Southern Jersey wilderness. Others were Tories, British sympathizers escaping the witch hunt following the War of Independence.

There were Germans, Scots, Irish, Swedes, Finns, Dutch and some fishermen from the New England coastal settlements such as Plymouth who followed the whales South and decided to stay. Early Quakers and Catholics came fleeing religious persecutions in their homelands. Germans lost themselves in the wilderness to avoid compulsory military duty in the constant wars among the German states. Later, Russian Jews also seeking a new life and freedom cleared land for farms and established the still existing villages of Woodbine, Mizpah and Rosenhayn, and the vanished settlements of Zion, Garton Road, Six Points and Hebron, all within the Southern Jersey pine belt. Other Russians established such tiny communities as Cassville.

Many later arrivals found jobs in the bog iron and glass furnaces. Others existed on the fruits of farming, berry picking and charcoal burning.

The vast woodlands were a place in which one could pursue one's own chosen life style without question, and where life flowed as easily and as silently as the area's deep streams. There was considerable community sharing. There was also suspicion, and still is, of outsiders.

At one time, because of the wild imaginations of sensation seeking writers, there was a stigma to the word "Piney." Today's Pine Barrens residents boast of their status. One told me, "I'm a bona fide Piney—I got to be. My folks lived around here so long I guess they were acquainted with the Lenape. Might even be one in the family."

Chatsworth is the unofficial "Capital" of the Pines. Lo-

The Kirby lumber mill, located on Church Road in Medford Township. This photo, made by William Cooper of Medford in 1916 on a glass plate negative, shows the mill complex which had grown from the original 1778 Haines Mill. Lumber was big business in the Pines.

cated in Woodland Township, in Burlington County, only three miles off highway Route 72, it has a population about 300, a general store, a gas station and a post office. It was originally known as Shamong Station. The town took its present name in 1900.

The greed of civilization has always been at the door of the Barrens. The iron masters looked upon the woods as a means of keeping their furnaces blazing; likewise the glass men. When a section of timber was depleted, another was tackled until the wooded sections began disappearing at an alarming rate. The death of the iron industry in the 1850s saved the remaining trees, although charcoal makers for many years after caused their share of destruction.

In the late 1800s the Pines were again threatened when industrialist Joseph Wharton of Philadelphia acquired 90,000 acres, intending to tap the enormous watershed and sell its water to the city of Philadelphia. His plan was thwarted when state legislators became aware of the dangers and prohibited the transfer of New Jersey water to Pennsylvania. Frustrated, Wharton's heirs sold their holdings to the state in 1953. The land was immediately marked for public use.

Not more than two years ago the Barrens faced another crisis when the construction of a giant jetport was under consideration. Developers grabbed for land, regardless of historical or ecological considerations. Faced with the realization that the Barrens could become another asphalt jungle, environmentalists and just plain concerned citizens banded together and made their voices heard in Trenton, and eventually Washington.

On September 25, 1979, the U.S. Interior Department announced the first federal purchases under the Pinelands Preservation Act, in which the federal government, in cooperation with the state of New Jersey, launched a drive

The thriving glass works center of Crowleytown on the
Mullica River is today a picturesque natural area deep
within the Pine Barrens. *(George M. Abbott photo)*

to preserve the vast wilderness area for generations to come. At the present writing, the battle is on in the courts in an attempt to break down the Act's building restrictions; several plans for large developments are waiting in the wings and no-one can predict the final outcome with any degree of confidence.

The Pine Barrens is of historical as well as ecological importance. It is also home to some of South Jersey's greatest legends and folklore, as well as a colorful array of characters all of whom in their own way have added priceless chapters to the folk heritage of the state.

It is with the legends and lore of the Pines that this book is concerned. The spectrum is so wide, however, that this effort represents only a small fraction of the tales available.

I would like to have made this collection more complete, if such a thing is possible, or at least larger. But a feeling of urgency compels me to publish this manuscript now because as the song says, "the times they are a-changin'." Many of my good friends in the Pines have passed on, and too many others are old-timers with failing memories. With their departure from the scene, an era will have ended whose flavor cannot ever be recaptured.

Sammy and His Fiddle

Folk writers have long been fascinated with the ancient legend in which an old man bargains with the devil, his soul for a return to youth. It has appeared in many forms, in many lands, including two operatic versions.

The Southern Jersey Pinelands story tellers have their own version of this tale. It concerns the Giberson family, who were pioneers in the Ocean County and Little Egg Harbor regions of the Pines. Many of the Gibersons still reside in the area.

Samuel Gordon Giberson, one of the well-known clan who lived deep in the woodlands of Ocean County during the middle 1800s, was known throughout the area as "Fiddler Sammy Buck." Every door was open to him and his fiddle. Sammy had two joys in life: to play for the social gatherings of his Pines neighbors and to enjoy a nip or two, preferably two, in the taverns of the area.

One night at a small backwoods inn near New Gretna, Sammy and another character by the name of Bill Denn began swapping tales over a few bolts of Jersey Lightnin' (Pineland applejack) and doing a bit of bragging. Eventually a dispute arose as to who was the better fiddler and dancer.

They decided on a contest. Sammy played for Denn while the latter displayed his dancing skill, and Denn played fiddle for Sammy. As the night progressed, so did the drinking and dancing until finally Sammy boasted, "I can beat you or any man I ever seed dancin' and fiddlin'. Could even beat the devil in a showdown."

The contest ended inconclusively, with both participants exhausted. Sammy weaved out of the tavern and along the road to his shack. As he approached a bridge he stopped for a nip from his flask, as a precaution against the morning damps. A dark figure blocked his way.

"Sammy Giberson?" asked the stranger.

"Yeh," replied the tired and slightly tipsy Sammy.

"I hear you think you can beat me dancing and fiddling?" said the figure on the bridge.

Considering this a challenge, Sammy replied, "I can beat anybody. Who are you?"

"The devil. Start playing!"

According to the tale repeated many times in the woodlands, Sammy took out his fiddle and started a tune. The devil began dancing. The more he danced the wilder became the music and the steps. Then it was Sammy's turn. The contest continued to dawn.

Apparently an understanding was reached in which the devil promised Sammy to teach him tunes that no one else knew or could play, including an "air tune," and Sammy would become the greatest fiddler the Pines had ever known, or would ever know.

Giberson continued to delight the Pinelands with new and fancy fiddling, including tricks of playing he had never attempted before. He'd fiddle with the instrument above his head, behind his back, even on the ground. One of his favorite tricks to astonish listeners was to remove violin strings one by one until only a single one remained. Sammy could play as expertly and as beautifully upon the single string as upon the normal four. He was always well supplied with refreshment during these performances, the termination of which varied according to Sammy's mood of the moment.

Following Sammy's encounter on the bridge that one early morning, listeners detected something different about their favorite musician. He was not only playing strange tunes but given to telling tales of a close association with a creature he called the devil. According to the Pines people, Sammy would disappear on moonlight nights and from the deep woods would come the sounds of not one, but two fiddles! These became known as the devil duets.

Sammy Giberson soon began to feel his oats and play games on his duet partner, every so often slipping in a well-known hymn tune while they were playing. At this, the devil was forced to stop fiddling and vanish.

No one knows for sure the final outcome of this strange relationship. Sammy continued playing for the Pinelanders, especially the much requested "air tune," which Giberson would inform one and all he "just picked outta the air." This he would not perform unless well fortified with his special brew and then, according to stories told by listeners, he would rise to the heights of a Paganini. Although many tried to copy the "air tune," none could master it. Sammy would ignore requests for this melody until a late hour. As soon as he played it, he would end his performance, pack his fiddle, and disappear into the woodlands.

Eventually Sammy died. According to some reports he is buried in a Little Egg Harbor Township woods cemetery. To those with livelier imaginations, Sammy still roams the Pines. Recalling the legend that the devil never gave any-

thing without demanding something in return, many believe that Satan finally collected Sammy as payment for his fiddle lessons.

The fiddle itself was locked in its black box and put upon an attic shelf. From time to time, some say, it would break into melody of its own accord, an added embellishment to the folklore that has sprung up around Sammy. Whether that is true or not, we do know that the fiddle eventually vanished.

However, those who frequent Pineland trails during brisk autumn evenings when the leaves begin to turn, swear they still hear the sounds of Sammy and his fiddle playing the "air tune."

Or is it just the night winds among the trees?

Note: Sammy Giberson actually lived in the woodlands of what is now Ocean County, (Ocean County was formed from Burlington County in 1850), and was well known to the folk thereabouts for his fiddling abilities. According to Burlington County records, Sammy was born in that county, perhaps at Barnegat or Tuckerton. No one knows for sure. His date of birth is given as September 16, 1808. His burial spot remains in question.

The White Stag of Shamong

Quaker Bridge, deep in the Jersey Pines about six miles
from the iron village of Batsto and four miles from Atsion,
is the setting for one of the legends of the Pinelands that
has flourished for more than one hundred years.

In the 1700s, Quaker Bridge was the point at which
devout Gloucester County Quakers crossed the Batsto
River on their way to Monthly Meeting at Tuckerton. This
was a dangerous practice, the Batsto having been much
wider and wilder at that time than it is now. Some of those
attempting the crossing, hampered by heavy clothing, were
caught in the current and swept away with their horses.

This led to a meeting of Gloucester Quakers with those
of Burlington County in 1772. Following a long discussion,
it was agreed that together they would erect a bridge of
cedar logs at the favorite cross-over point of the river.
This they did, and the place thereafter became known as
Quaker Bridge.

The sandy road hacked out of the Pines by the Friends
soon became a route for stages and Jersey Wagons con-
necting with the Long-a-Coming Trail from Haddonfield.
This part of the Pines was known by the Lenni Lenape
Indians as Shamong, or Oschummo, and is the setting for a
strange tale of the great white buck.

This was told to me by a native of the area when we were
both trapped by a sudden storm, and forced to spend the
night in his small cabin near Pleasant Mills.

According to the story-teller, it was just such a storm as
we were experiencing that had overtaken a stage coach
deep in the sandy trail leading to Quaker Bridge. Although
blinded by the heavy rain and approaching darkness, and
fearful of being mired in the ever-deepening ruts of the
road, the stage driver attempted to go ahead and try to
reach one of the taverns ahead.

As the stage and its frightened passengers approached Quaker Bridge, a great white stag loomed in the center of the road. The horses reared in fright and refused to go ahead. They pawed the ground and tried to break from harness. Fastening the reins to the stage, the driver jumped to the ground, rifle in hand. As he did so, the white stag vanished as suddenly as it had appeared!

Together with a couple of the more daring passengers, he walked ahead to where the white stag had been standing. To the astonishment of all, they discovered that the bridge across the river had been washed away by the storm. Had it not been for the great stag, the coach and all aboard it would have plunged into the swollen stream!

Visibly shaken by their experience and drenched by the storm, the men returned to what small shelter the stage could afford them to await the morning light and make their way back slowly to Haddonfield. Their story quickly spread throughout the Pinelands, where it is still repeated today.

No hunter would dare take a shot at a white stag from that time on.

The Man who Rode a Fish

Tennessee had its Davey Crockett, Kentucky its Daniel Boone, and New Jersey had Jonas Cattell.

A real folk hero of South Jersey, Cattell was born in 1758 on a farm called "Lavender Hills," just outside Woodbury in what is now Deptford Township. From his early youth until his death at the age of 96, Cattell had a minute knowledge of the nearby woodlands and the creatures which inhabited them. In fact, he is the man who cut several of the early Pinelands trails.

Woodlands scout, New Jersey Revolutionary War hero, blacksmith, long distance runner and gifted tall tale teller, Cattell continues to fascinate and bemuse local historians. His real exploits and his tall stories were so intermingled that today there is many a conflict as to which was which. It is certainly true that a good number of his physical feats have been authenticated.

The accomplishment that placed him in the realm of genuine historic heroes was a remarkable run from Haddonfield to Fort Mercer, to warn the American troops that the Hessians were on their way to attack. Under the command of Colonel Carl von Donop, the Hessians had encamped at Haddonfield and were planning an early morning surprise attack on the fort. Cattell slipped through the lines, and his outstanding running endurance combined with a detailed knowledge of backwoods trails made it possible for him to reach Colonel Christopher Greene at Fort Mercer well ahead of the enemy.

His warning allowed the revolutionary garrison time to prepare a successful defense which, as every New Jersey history scholar knows, ended in the rout and almost complete annihilation of the Hessian attackers. Although he later served in the Continental forces, Cattell's run was his greatest war exploit. He was eighteen at the time.

Following the war, Jonas Cattell returned home and for a time became guide and "whipper-in" of the Gloucester Fox Hunting Club. Here, according to his own stories, his hunting methods were quite unique. Spurning the use of horses—"my own legs are better"—Jonas would beat the mounted men to the kill every time. Hunters riding up would be greeted with, "What took yuh so long?"

On a wager, Jonas went on foot from Woodbury to Cape Island (now Cape May City) in one day, to deliver a letter. He also brought back the reply, completing a journey of 160 miles on foot in two days.

Before starting on a run, the six foot tall Cattell would breakfast on eggs or raw meat. His attire has been described as consisting of a red flannel shirt, heavy overcoat, waterproof shoes or fisherman's boots, and canvas leggings tied above his hips. He carried a gun and an Indian tomahawk in his various adventures.

Many years after his death, Jonas Cattell figured in the annual Champion Liar Contest held by Atlantic City's famous Tuna Club. Assemblyman Hugh Mehorter won the prize with what is still considered to be the tallest tale of the South Jersey woodlands and streams.

According to the Honorable Gentleman, Jonas was sailing a small craft down Big Timber Creek one day when an eighteen-foot sturgeon jumped aboard and swamped it. As the big, mean-looking fish sprang overboard, Jonas, who was floundering in the rising water, seized it by the gills and clasped his legs tightly around the creature. The sturgeon made for deeper water and Cattell stayed with it, riding it like a bucking bronco in the best rodeo style.

Man and fish raced downstream toward Big Timber Bridge. As they came abreast of the span, Jonas threw one leg around a post, but could not hold on. By this time he felt that his personal honor was at stake, and he was determined to ride his sea-going bronc to the very ocean, if necessary.

At Eagle Point, Cattell ran his steed ashore, and the amazing ride was over. Like a good fisherman, Jonas enjoyed the fight but cared little for the catch, which he threw back into the stream—a shame, some say, for it has been a while since eighteen-foot long sturgeon have been seen in these waters.

And whom do we have as the authority for this tale? None other than Jonas Cattell himself, who never balked at telling it and others equally as wild, according to Mrs. Kurt Hoelle of Woodbury. She has made quite a study of Cattell and his exploits, and has shared with me the tale of a race he had with an Indian, from Mount Holly to Woodbury. Naturally, Jonas, who admitted to fifty years of age at the time, beat the Indian. Mrs. Hoelle never could find out the age of the red man!

Jonas Cattell died in 1854 at the age of 96. His grave is located in a tiny wooded grove in Deptford Township. The Deptford Kiwanis Club keeps his memory alive with a yearly tribute in the form of a long distance run from Haddonfield to Fort Mercer, and other activities.

Strange Encounter

I have spent considerable time on the back trails of the Pines, seeking some of the forgotten towns so eloquently brought to life by the late Dr. Henry C. Beck and at the same time attempting to discover new ones of my own.

In the course of these pursuits I thought I'd take a fling at the pirate lore of the area. Down near the marshes of Lower Bank on one of these hikes, I explored a sandy path leading back into the tangled brush that lines the Mullica (formerly the Little Egg Harbor) River.

I had not gone far when I discovered a rough, board shanty which seemed to have a semblance of life about it. Not wishing to be greeted by buckshot, as sometimes happens when one wanders uninvited into private diggings in the Pines, I hailed the occupant before venturing too close.

He turned out to be a man well into his 60s, bearded, with white, wind-blown hair, heavy woolen shirt (it was getting toward fall) and trousers tucked carelessly into boots. As expected, he carried an ever-ready shotgun, but laid it aside when he apparently decided I was harmless.

After formal greetings I explained my wanderings.

"Well," he said, in the slow twangy voice typical of the Southern Jersey Pines, "you came to the right place. The Little Egg has had its share of pirates. Some of the stories are true, I suspect, others are just so many hand-me-downs. You can believe or disbelieve as you choose. Around here no-one forces you to do nothin'." And he ended with a chuckle, "We don't do nothin' but fish, pick a few berries and feed the deer. Not much else to do anyway."

Andy, whom I will not identify further because, like many others of the deep Pines, he preferred to live undisturbed, asked nothing more of life than that the river supply his fish and the land support a garden patch to take care of the vegetables. For store-bought essentials, he picked up a few bucks from gathering pine cones for the florists and helping with cranberry picking in season.

He was born in the Pines. His folk were strawberry pickers in the spring and cranberry harvesters in the fall, working in the bogs. He was one of several children, all of whom had moved away. Andy stayed of his own choice.

He had a deep religious feeling for the great wilderness that had nothing to do with church-going religion, and was steeped in tales of pirates, Indians, robbers and war deserters.

"I have seen many strange things back here myself and don't rightly think we should doubt tales of the old folk. I could tell you things you won't believe.

"You say you doubt pirates were ever 'round here? Well, I won't swear they were or they weren't, but out in that drowned land (swamps) you hear some strange sounds and see strange shadows. According to some folk, the pirate with the big black beard—Blackbeard, that's what they called him, a real mean cuss—used one of the islands up-river as a hangout. Story is he buried treasure around here somewhere. Every spring folk come out here and start a-diggin'. As far as I heard it, they ain't found nothin'."

Andy also recalled that another tale handed down from prior generations of Pine woods settlers is that New Jersey Tories, and there were many, fleeing the witch hunt that followed the surrender of General Cornwallis at Yorktown, buried their silverware and other treasures deep in the Pines, until such time as it was safe to reclaim them. There is no accurate record as to whether any returned and, if so, whether they found their buried belongings.

History also records that following the first battle of Trenton many Hessian mercenaries sought safety in the woods and swamps and stayed there, accounting for some of the original Piney families.

I left Andy with the promise of an early return. He was standing by his unpainted board door still smoking his ever-present pipe, as I made my way back to more familiar paths.

Returning some weeks later, I again sought my old-timer and found the shack easily enough, but no Andy. There seemed to be no sign of recent occupation. The door was hanging from one hinge and torn rags waved from a glass-less window.

Puzzled, I left, and continued up toward Batsto where I chanced to run into a fire warden. Striking up a conversation, I asked about Andy.

"Oh, you mean the old Piney who lived down by Lower Bank? A real character. He died last year. There was nothing of value in his shack, so it was left as is. Guess it is burned down by now," the warden commented, adding, "lot of fires around here lately."

I protested that this was not possible as I had spoken with the man only a few weeks past.

"I can prove it," I persisted. "I have a whole conversation on my tape recorder. Here, listen."

I switched it on, the spindles turned, and the warden and I regarded each other uneasily. The tape was blank. Finally, he walked away and I had to accept the fact that this is the Pinelands!

A Matter of Crows, High Water and a Loose Head

The site of Hanover Furnace, Pemberton Township, Burlington County, is now within the bounds of Fort Dix. It was one of the earliest bog iron operations of the Pinelands, dating to 1791.

There were several owners and managers. One day during the time of Richard Jones as head man of the furnace in the late 1700s, Jerry Munyhon (or Monahan) and two companions, Dick Highbuck and Jack Matches, came looking for work. Matches told all who would listen that his companion Jerry was a wizard.

In the Pinelands vocabulary, this was akin to claiming connections with the Lower Regions. Judging from the variety of stories about Jerry, and there are hundreds, he either had this dark connection or was a clever trickster and illusionist.

Furnace operator Jones, according to our story tellers, refused Jerry a job, and the latter promised Jones he would be sorry for his refusal. A few minutes later the stack of the furnace began to billow black smoke and the fires were threatened with extinction. A flock of crows clogged the stack!

Munyhon told Jones that he had caused the crows to appear, and that unless Jones gave him work, they would stay. Jones relented. Jerry gave a signal and the crows flew away. The stack was unclogged and the furnace returned to normal function.

This was one of many tales of magic attributed to Munyhon.

One of his favorite tricks was to convince women that they were wading in rising waters, so they would hike their dresses. This mischief caused much embarrassment to the ladies involved.

Munyhon is also said to have had the knack of changing

things to appear what they were not. One of my informants, Adam Richards, said that on the way to a nearby store to buy provisions, Munyhon would fill his pockets with clam shells. He would make his purchases paying the storekeeper in bright, silver coins. However, after Munyhon had disappeared and the storekeeper again opened his money drawer, he found only clam shells!

This did not add to the wizard's popularity, nor did he make friends among the farmers by causing livestock to be mired in muddy streams, rescuing them (for a fee) with a wave of his hand.

Munyhon was fond of his brew and is said to have had a walking stick he could order to go fetch him liquor and an axe that would do his work for him. Charcoal-burning was big business in the Pines in the 1800s. Wood was always needed for charcoal pits. Jerry would hire himself out with others to chop trees for these fires, taking along two axes. His companions, always a bit afraid of his mysterious powers that would assert themselves without warning, left him pretty much to himself, and would go off in another direction.

Soon they would hear the sound of two axes chopping away, but Munyhon would be sunning himself beneath a tree. He invariably turned up with more cut wood than any of his companions. This sounds like another Paul Bunyan tale and possibly could be, but those woodcutters swore to the truth of their experience and their tales still have wide circulation all the way from Browns Mills south to Weymouth.

Topping all tales is the one in which Jerry went to a cabin in the woods near Hanover, a woodchopper's shack, and demanded food. When the woman of the house turned him down, he made her dance until she complied with his wishes. Then, not being satisfied, Jerry asked that she cut his hair. This she refused to do, brushing past him to go to the spring to fetch water. When she returned, Jerry had his head in his lap, between his knees, and was cutting his own hair! The startled housewife began screaming and the men folk came running, but by then Jerry had restored his head and returned to the brush.

What finally happened to Munyhon no-one seems to know. Like so many of the fabled characters of the Pines, he just disappeared. None living today actually saw Jerry, but recited these tales as having been handed down from father and grandfather.

They all warn, however, that if someone knocks on your door, head in his hands, and asks for a meal, don't refuse him. It's definitely bad luck.

The Ole Jersey Devil

In the full of an Autumn moon near the marshes and woodlands of Leeds Point in Atlantic County, you may suddenly come face to face with a strange creature, half bird, half horse and all devil!

If you relate your terrifying experience to a native, he will inform you that you have just encountered the famous Jersey Devil, who has been haunting these woodlands for more than 200 years. To some he is a destructive creature; to others just a poor being trying to be friendly.

According to legend, there was a certain Mrs. Leeds of Estellville (never further identified) who, finding she was "expecting" for the thirteenth time, in anger shouted, "I hope this time it's a devil!" The story relates that the child arrived, a baby devil, with horns, the face of a horse, batlike wings and a long tail. It gave a screech as midwives fled the room in terror. Then, unfolding its wings, it flew out the window and into the adjacent swamp. Those attending Mrs. Leeds raced to their homes, bolted doors, spread holy water on walls and lighted candles.

From here the story becomes confused. One version is that the new-born imp made its home in the swamp, raiding nearby chicken coops for food, causing the milk of cows to go sour, and generally disrupting farm life in the vicinity.

The braver of the local men formed posses to either shoot or capture it. They returned without accomplishing their end. Shortly afterward, the devil was reported sighted in the woods of Gloucester County near Woodbury, then up into what is now Burlington, and finally back in present-day Atlantic County, where it made its new home in the marshes of Leeds Point.

Mrs. Leeds and her brood of twelve children seem to have completely dropped out of history, although the Leeds name is a prominent family one in South Jersey.

The Jersey Devil has appeared from time to time in sightings which seem to herald the outbreak of war, according to those steeped in its study. It was reported seen just before the Spanish-American War, and in 1935, prior to events leading to World War II. The electronic age seems to have sent it into permanent hiding. It apparently did not announce the Korean or Vietnamese conflicts, perhaps agreeing with the politicians that they were merely "actions," not all-out war.

There are many versions of the Jersey Devil's birth, other than the most repeated one. In their book *The Jersey Devil,* James F. McCloy and Ray Miller, Jr., cite a gypsy curse (1850) involving a young Jersey girl who refused food to a gypsy. Another tale is that a clergyman passing through put a curse on Mrs. Leeds, because she refused to feed him at her home and slammed a door in his face.

South Jersey historian Alfred Heston reported in his *Jersey Waggon Jaunts* that the devil-child returned to his place of birth and sat on the back fence of the homestead. Mrs. Leeds, frightened, would not open her door and the "thing" finally flew away to the marshes of Leeds Point.

There are discrepancies regarding the birthplace of the Jersey Devil. These seem to depend on whether the story-teller is himself a resident of eastern or western Atlantic County. The late Henry Charlton Beck claimed that a Leeds Point woman showed him the wreckage of a house she said was the one from which the creature made his first flight. Leeds Point and Estellville are on opposite sides of the county, with plenty of Pinelands between, not to mention a county seat at Mays Landing, a race course, a gigantic airport and a state college!

Then there is the popular legend that Commodore Stephen Decatur, hero of the war with the Barbary Coast pirates, desired to test cannonballs being made at Hanover

Iron Works once located at what is now the confines of Ft. Dix. He is reported to have seen a batlike creature flying about and to have placed a cannonball right through it, without halting its flight.

A Philadelphian once offered $500 for the Devil, claiming it was a rare Australian vampire. This set off a number of search parties, much to the discomfort of Leeds Point residents. All returned empty handed. The exhibit of a stuffed animal alleged to have been the Devil at a Philadelphia museum proved to be a gross fake.

The South Jersey creature, also known as the Leeds Devil, was given official status as the State Demon in a 1939 guide book published by the W.P.A. The book boldly declared that the devil's favorite dish was Jersey ham and eggs, and that it spent Sunday mornings with a certain Atlantic County judge discussing "Republican politics." The author of *South Jersey Towns* points out that the book in question was written under the patronage of a Democratic administration, thus bringing into some question the veracity of the statement.

In 1966 the Jersey Devil was proposed for a postage stamp in a folklore series. The U.S. Post Office Department didn't take kindly to the idea.

However, the devil is preserved in fame by a South Jersey cocktail appropriately named "The Jersey Devil." Its base is the cranberry juice of the area, applejack, plus rums. A drinking companion of the author has expressed the opinion that this cocktail was responsible for some of the "sightings." It seems possible.

Nevertheless, a motorist on the Garden State Parkway not too many years ago reported to the State Police that "something" began running alongside his car right after he hit the Pine belt. And a troop of Boy Scouts in the

Wharton State Forest officially reported a strange creature near their camp.

As recently as 1974, two research students with electronic gear spent a couple of autumn nights in the Leeds Point woods, searching for the Jersey Devil. They were driven out by mosquitos, whom they concluded were the real Jersey Devils.

Wooden sculpture of the Jersey Devil created out of driftwood by Geni Alles of Bargaintown.

Apprentice of Barnegat

Stories of pirates and their gold are among the many interesting legends told and retold in the Southern Jersey Pines whenever men gather for a sip of Jersey brew.

Among the most popular of these tales is the story of William Bennett. Described as a rough seaman type, with bushy, long hair and a thick black beard, Bennett appeared near mainland Barnegat in Ocean County in the early 1700s, built himself a shanty, and spent his days fishing, hunting and berry picking.

He kept strictly to the prevailing Piney code, never mingled, disappeared into the woods if anyone approached his habitat, and finally died alone in his sparsely furnished shack.

According to legend he is buried in the nearby pines. The same legend connects him directly with more exciting things that happened across the sea in England.

The notorious Captain William Kidd, former English naval officer turned pirate, was captured in May, 1701, off the New England coast of America, returned to London and tried for piracy at the Old Bailey. Ten of his crew were also put on trial.

Seven were found guilty and hanged along with their captain. Three more were declared innocent and escaped the hangman because they pleaded that they had been sold as apprentices to Captain Kidd, and under English law were forced to do his bidding, right or wrong.

Their pleas of innocence were worthy of a Gilbert and Sullivan opera plot, but they impressed the court, and there were tears in the eyes of attendants, according to contemporary reports of the trial. Thus Robert Lumley, William Jenkins and Richard Varlicorn, the lucky three, were released and told to sin no more.

What happened to two of the men is unknown. The

third, William Jenkins, returned to America and headed
for the Jersey coast, some say, to search for gold Captain
Kidd is alleged to have buried on the shore. Others say that
Jenkins just desired to forget the whole episode and have
the world forget him. But Jersey legend has it that Bennett
and Jenkins were the same man. The place where he built
his shack came to be known as Bennett's Neck, located
about a mile south of Barnegat on the main Shore Road to
Manahawkin.

Some people tramping the woodlands in that vicinity
have reported seeing a shadowy figure apparently searching for something. Could it be pirate gold?

The Girl He Left Behind

Another, more romantic, Captain Kidd legend of the Pines concerns the girl he left behind.

The waters of Great Bay, Grassy Bay, Reed's and Little Bay are said to have been favorite haunts of the infamous pirate.

It was while in these waters awaiting repairs to his ship that he became infatuated of a farm lass identified only as Amanda, who lived in the vicinity of Barnegat. Because of this attachment, Kidd planned to abandon the wild, seafaring life of a buccaneer, trading it for the more peaceful one of a coastal fisherman.

With this in mind he is said to have spirited away a great amount of stolen treasure from under the eyes of his crew with whom, according to pirate code, he should have shared it, and buried it in the vicinity of Oyster Creek.

The love story could have had a peaceful and happy conclusion at this point save that some of Kidd's pirate crew became aware of their captain's amour and, believing they were being abandoned, they jumped ship and made their way overland to New York.

Given the promise of full pardons, they informed authorities of the whereabouts of the pirate captain and his vessel. Kidd's ship was anchored near the mouth of the Little Egg Harbor river when three British armed vessels closed in on him. In a running battle he made good his escape into open waters.

His luck did not hold in a later encounter off the New England coast, as we have already mentioned.

Amanda vanished into the vastness of the Pines. Whether she ever dug up the treasure and used it will never be known. It could still be deep in the earth, guarded by the ghostly figures who roam these woods and marshes.

The Rabbit Woman

The Pines had their share of witches, real or fancied, such as Peggy Clevenger up Pasadena way, who according to legend could turn herself into a rabbit at will.

One of these tales relates that on a certain afternoon a dog was chasing a rabbit which jumped through the open window of Peggy's house, located about five miles from Mt. Misery. Suddenly, in place of the rabbit, there was Peggy looking out the window while the dog ran off yelping into the woods as if demons were after him.

Another favorite Peggy Clevenger story concerns a neighbor who was forced to climb a rail fence to reach a road near her property. Every time she tried, there would be a big green lizard sitting on the fence defying her. Finally gathering her nerve, she picked up a large stone and flung it at the reptile, hitting it on the head. The next day Peggy Clevenger was sporting a black eye!

Peggy was alleged to have had a stocking full of gold which she kept in her frame house. (No one explains how she got it.) When one of the frequent Pines fires raced through the settlement, her house was destroyed in the flames. Peggy was found dead within.

Despite thorough searches, no stocking of gold has ever been found. But whenever the tale is repeated to a new generation, there is renewed digging activity in the vicinity.

Dr. Herbert N. Halpert, the noted folklorist, disputes the fire story. He was told by a Piney that Peggy was killed for her gold by a man named Bill Mullen, another Piney, who confessed the crime on his deathbed.

Mullen also failed to find the gold!

A Tale of the Beach

The upper reaches of Brigantine Beach, still a desolate stretch of high sand dunes, hermit crabs and tall grasses, are great for surf-fishing. This is a sport in which you stand up to your waist in ice-cold water, take biting salt spray in your face, and cast out a line hoping that some unsuspecting fish will be seeking dinner closer to the breaker line, rather than further to sea. It's also an activity that sometimes brings out most unlikely characters, like the bewhiskered individual who told me the story of the captain of the mists.

In the days of sail, the waters off Brigantine Island were known as the "graveyard of the Jersey shore." The sands of the beach were strewn with parts of proud craft which had crashed on the treacherous reefs during the frequent nor'easters that attack the island. Public pressure eventually resulted in the establishment of a life-saving station on the upper reaches of the beach, but not until hundreds of men, women and children rested in hastily dug and unmarked graves.

My weather-beaten companion, who had wandered down from another part of the beach, took to reminiscing about these wrecks of yesteryear and he spoke about a strange dark figure which many times appeared in the front of a coming storm, warning any who lingered to make for higher ground. According to certain old-timers, this was the captain of one of the wrecked vessels. He would appear in the gathering swirl of the storm, apparently shouting his warnings, although his voice was lost in the rising winds.

Some say the figure was dressed in a flapping sou'easter already soaked with rain; others report that he appeared in a black cloak tightly wrapped around him, with no headgear and his wild hair whipped by the wind. There was terror on his features as if he had already seen the deadly results of just such a storm.

Encounters with the captain were reported a number of times during the early part of the century. My story teller—sorry, I never got his name—had not actually seen the figure himself. "But strange things are possible on a beach in a storm," he concluded somberly, reeling in his line and disappearing up the beach in the gathering dusk.

As the breakers seemed suddenly to be crashing with greater intensity, and a breeze was whipping itself into what could become a more serious blow, I also reeled in and headed for home. I had no yearning to encounter our misty captain.

Results of the day: no fish, but one good yarn.

Historic Note: Burying wreck victims in unmarked graves was common practice along the Jersey coast in the 1800s. One such trench grave exists in the old Quaker cemetery at Smithville, just up the road from Leeds Point and the back waters of Brigantine Island. On April 15, 1854, the packet ship *Powhatan* went aground off Brigantine in a storm. Everyone aboard perished. Forty bodies washed ashore and were buried at Rum Point (now a casino). Other bodies were taken to Smithville by Isaac and Robert Smith, wrapped in sheets provided by the women of the village and buried in a trench. They were never identified.

Visitor with a Lantern

Many of the older houses in the Pinelands and its environs are by tradition playgrounds for a variety of mysterious creatures which go bump in the night. They are usually easily able to make their way in the total darkness in which we humans grope and stumble.

But every so often, one of the nighttime prowlers needs an assist from earthly progress and science. Such a one is he who walks along a certain creek in Clermont, an old stage coach town in the backwoods of Cape May County, carrying a lantern to light his way.

The Jeremiah Hand home in Clermont, built about 1790, figured in this tale. One of the occupants of the house in the 1800s was a man by the name of John Dobbs. He was walking along a creek which today bears his name, swinging a lantern to light his way, when a shotgun blast rang out. Dobbs was killed; his assailant never was found.

Soon it became whispered about the neighborhood that John made return visits to his former home, moving things about just to be annoying. As late as 1910, tenants were moving in and out of the house with great regularity because of Johnny's alleged goings-on.

Then Mrs. William Cherry moved into the house in 1911, despite the tales of unusual activity there. Not being a timid soul, she decided to corner the ghostly visitor who apparently amused himself by running about the attic and making cracking noises.

One night Mrs. Cherry sat herself on the stair leading to the loft, which was unfurnished and approachable only through a trap door. She did not have to wait long. The cracking sounds started; the padding footsteps increased. Mrs. Cherry threw up the trap door and came face to face with her ghost.

It was a chipmunk! It seems that the creature had stored

walnuts in the loft, and on cold evenings he would roll them about on the floor to break the shells. Mrs. Cherry and her "ghostly" visitor became friends, and she stayed at the house until 1915.

I was relating the story to a newcomer to the vicinity who countered. "That's fine, but what about the man with the lantern? He is no chipmunk." Not having met said stroller in person I had to leave this one unanswered. But of late years Johnny and his lantern seem to have disappeared. Perhaps the growing cost of lamp oil made the nightly strolls too costly.

Pasadena and the Boiling Well

Pasadena, New Jersey? Correct!

A group of farm homes in the deep Pines of Ocean County, near Whitesbog, Pasadena has a lonesome air, and that is how the residents like it. About the only time there is any action is during hunting season, since these are good deer woods and many hunting lodges are located in the vicinity.

There is a sign off Route 72 that points to Pasadena. There are also a number of signs along the sandy road that say "Keep Out." It's not that the folks are unfriendly; they just don't hanker for too many visitors and prefer to be undisturbed, which of course is entirely in keeping with Piney philosophy. Another reason for the "Keep Out" signs, according to one native I talked with, is "to keep danged hunters outta my property, cause some don't know the difference between a deer, a cow and a hog."

Pasadena is an area with natural clay pits. During the 1840s and 1850s there were two terra-cotta pipe factories located there, manufacturing drain pipes and bricks. The remains of one, the Union Clay Works, is still to be found deep in the woodlands, almost hidden in the creeping vegetation.

The decline of these operations can be traced to a lack of adequate transportation facilities, as well as the ever-dwindling amount of wood available for pit fires. As plants closed, people began to move away, until only small plot farmers remained. At the time, Pasadena was still a major stop along a stagecoach route from Mount Holly to Tuckerton. Despite this, the community was rapidly reduced to a handful of families.

Some contended that the curse of the Pine Witch and the Pine Wizard was on the place; of course, those remaining scoffed at these stories.

There is also a local tale that when fire destroyed one of the brick and pipe factories, the bodies of a man and a woman were found in the ashes. Never identified, they were buried in an unmarked grave. Legend has them returning to their last rendezvous from time to time, as ghostly shadows.

Pasadena is also said to have been the site of an eerie boiling well, on land belonging to Peggy Clevenger and her husband Bill, around whom many Piney legends are woven. According to the story, when Bill, who liked his drinking and brawling, felt he was about to die, he told Peggy that if things in the other world were as hot as the preachers said they were, he would let her know. Sure enough the night after Bill's death the family well began to bubble and steam. Many old-timers, mostly gone now, swore they saw the sizzling well. Its exact location, however, has never been pinpointed.

Pasadena is surrounded by legends even to its name. According to notes found in the archives of the Ocean County Library at Toms River, Pasadena is a combination of Indian names, put together by Dr. T. B. Elliot in the early 1800s by combining phonetic sounds.

Residents live comfortably with these legends which have been passed down through the generations along with their small patches of land. Their only fears are that developers will some day step in and disturb all the peaceful ghosts of the past. But then again, they have lived with these fears for years.

The Dancing Bandit

Although not as widely known as the headless horseman of Sleepy Hollow, the ghostly horseman of the Pines has been a legend in South Jersey for 200 years. He is said to be the dancing Pines robber Joseph Mulliner, about whom many stories are told.

Mulliner and his gang operated in the Barrens during the time of the American Revolution and made their headquarters in a swamp in the vicinity of what is now Egg Harbor City. At the forks of the Mullica there is a large oak tree with spreading branches, overlooking the water. According to local legend, it was from this tree that highwayman Joseph Mulliner was hanged and left to dangle, after his capture by a posse of patriots and farmers angered beyond tolerance by his raids upon their homes and lands. Some residents of nearby Sweetwater cut the body down, the legend continues, and buried it in a lonely spot beside the road leading to the village.

It has been reported on occasion that the thundering beat of a horse's hoofs has been heard along the road, and a lone celebrator returning from a party nearby told of hearing the hoofs and feeling a cold wind pass him by. Another ghostly legend tells of a rider in a long black cape emerging periodically from the dark waters of the Mullica, carrying its ashen faced head under an arm.

Mulliner was a tall, handsome, swaggering Englishman with a passion for elaborate uniforms, ornate swords and an ever present brace of pistols in his wide leather belt. He was a complex character who loved to dance and attend parties (uninvited, of course), all the while heading the worst bunch of cutthroats that ever infested the South Jersey woodlands.

Mulliner and his band of about forty men were supposedly loyal to King George III, but there is abundant evidence that they were loyal only to themselves. Tories as well as patriots suffered at their hands. But because of this so-called allegiance to the English crown, they were widely known by the name "refugees."

Taking advantage of the fact that all able bodied men were away, defending New Jersey as part of the Continental army in Trenton, New Brunswick, Monmouth and Princeton, Mulliner and his band would swoop down on an unprotected farm house, burning and pillaging without fear of resistance. Anything that could not be carried away was set afire.

However, when he was not engaged in plunder, Mulliner liked nothing better than to be the uninvited guest at social affairs in private homes and taverns of the area. A tale is told of how he learned of a wedding taking place at a tavern in old Washington (now a part of the Wharton Tract) and decided to invite himself to the festivities. Approaching the back of the place, he nearly tripped over a young girl lying on the grass, crying. When she saw the giant outlaw she ran for the building. Mulliner decided he'd better delay his appearance.

After a while he entered quietly, and stood at the rear of those gathered there. A wedding was in progress. The bride was none other than the girl he had encountered outside. Furthermore, the groom was an old foe who had boasted he would kill Mulliner on sight. The outlaw, feeling the girl was being forced into this marriage, gave a wild whoop, fired his two pistols in the air and sent the wedding guests scrambling for cover. In the excitement, the groom disappeared.

Mulliner replaced his pistols, assured everyone that he was there for no harm, and invited them all to eat and drink, leading the way himself. He also ordered the fiddler to play. After a few whirls around the floor with the reluctant bride-to-be, he backed out the door and jumped upon his horse, which had been held in readiness by a member of his band.

Here the tale ends without explanation as to what happened to the frightened bridegroom or the bride. We know Mulliner got away unharmed.

Another legend that always surfaces in any discussion of Mulliner concerns a raid by his gang, minus its leader, on a farm near Washington owned by a widow named Bates. Her four sons were serving in the Continental army.

According to the story, the marauders stole her pigs and poultry and then entered the house to cart away furniture and anything else of value they might find. Widow Bates attempted to fight them off so they took her, tied her to a nearby tree, and burned her home to the ground.

Neighbors rallied to her aid as they do in the Pines, and reconstructed the dwelling, even donating furniture and food. Mulliner, it was reported, had no prior knowledge of the raid and was upset by the actions of his men.

One morning, a bag of coins amounting to several hundred dollars was found hanging outside the Bates cabin window. It was always believed that these coins were placed there by Mulliner to show his disapproval of the actions of his followers. There is, of course, some doubt about the story.

Charles Peterson, a novelist of the 1800s, wrote a book about the American Revolution in South Jersey. He called it *Kate Aylesford*. The locale was in and around Pleasant Mills, Batsto and Sweetwater. So real did he paint his characters and so closely did he follow actual events, that many to this day believe there was a real-life Kate Aylesford. For many years the Elijah Clark mansion at Pleasant Mills was known as the Kate Aylesford House. One of the characters in the book was the outlaw Mulliner, who broke

The Elijah Clark mansion at Pleasant Mills, known as the Kate Aylesford House.

into a party at the mansion and danced with the pretty hostess, while his followers held other guests at gun point. No doubt some of the Mulliner legends had their beginnings with author Peterson.

It was his love of dancing and playing the dandy that led to Mulliner's undoing. When the British troops departed and the war ended, the men of South Jersey came home. Learning of the activities of Mulliner and his gang, they formed a company of rangers under an old Indian fighter named Captain Baylin, and went seeking the Pines robbers.

One night Mulliner, up to his usual tricks at an inn in New Columbia (now Nesco), was whirling the girls about the dance floor and drinking heavily. One of the men present slipped out a back way and contacted Captain Baylin, who arrived with his rangers, surrounded the place, captured Mulliner's guards and took the outlaw from the dance floor.

The rangers escorted their bound prisoner on a horse to Burlington and turned him over to the authorities there. Mulliner was placed in the Burlington jail, charged with banditry and treason. It did not take a court long to find him guilty. He was hanged in the yard of the prison in August, 1781. Without its leader, the gang scattered and peace once more reigned in the Pines.

An old Scotsman once told me, "Scotland had a glorious history until some danged historian came along and pointed out that it was mostly legend." So it goes with the story of Mulliner. We have seen from the above that the so-called hanging tree at the Forks never served that purpose, at least so far as Mulliner is concerned. His death came at the hands of legal authority after trial and conviction. Whether or not the body was brought back and buried at Sweetwater is also debatable.

According to historian Watson Buck, Mulliner's body was

indeed brought back from Burlington and interred along the Pleasant Mills-Nesco road. In 1850, he says, a party of drunken woodsmen from Batsto dug up the bones, but Jesse Richards, Batsto ironmaster, had them returned to their original resting place.

A gun club in the vicinity first marked the alleged grave with a wooden slab, and it now bears an official State historic sign. But there are skeptics who question what lies beneath the marker.

"I Owe My Soul. . ."

An early industrial institution in the South Jersey Pines was the company store, made famous in this day by singer Tennessee Ernie Ford in the line, "I owe my soul to the company store!"

This is no idle description of the store that sold everything to the worker on a credit basis against his earnings. Most times the money owed by the worker to the company was far in excess of what the company might owe him in wages. Consequently he was constantly in debt and had to keep to his job regardless of working conditions.

Many workers never saw actual currency. They were paid in credit slips or company money acceptable only at the company-run general store, usually conveniently located near the mill or forge which employed the laborers.

The manager of the operation kept a set of books showing hours worked by each individual, the rate of pay of each, and a short but to-the-point character analysis mainly concerned with whether the individual was sober or addicted to drinking bouts that would absent him from his

Money used at the Batsto company store by the iron workers. The issuance of scrip was common in the iron, glass and paper industries of early South Jersey.

job. A duplicate of this information was forwarded to the company store manager each week. This permitted the latter to keep records of who was to be given credit, how much, and what risks he, the store manager, might be taking with the boss's goods.

An example of the close tabs kept on work and workers is found in records such as those of the Weymouth store of 1813:

> April 5—Joseph Grant did not go to ore beds. Drinking last night; sick today. No credit.
> April 12—Joseph Pettit separated this life this morning. *(Which meant all credit stopped for family.)*
> April 20—John Brown discharged for setting woods on fire.

In some instances, especially with apprentices of the glass and iron factories, spoilage of materials caused by a young boy's lack of skill was charged against him. His credit at the end of a hard week was sometimes counted in pennies.

Foremen were tough. There was no appeal from their decisions. A worker who crossed a foreman found himself jobless and sometimes blacklisted if the foreman had friends in other nearby works. Separation from a job was physical at times, and the discharged employee had a black eye or sore jaw to show for his last session with the supervisor. On the other hand, the foreman had to be ever ready with his fists, as there were instances in which he could be the target of an angry worker armed with an iron bar or other weapon.

The company store system had both advantages and disadvantages. Among the former was the convenience to the housewife who lived with her family in a company house near the place her husband worked. (Rent was automatically deducted from the weekly wage.) She had no means of transportation to another location for shopping, assuming she had any actual money to spend. The company itself discouraged private endeavor. Consequently there were no nearby markets with which to compare prices. The company store handled everything from flour and meal to beds, blankets and patent medicines.

One of the oldest examples of a company store in South Jersey still in existence is located in the Batsto Village restoration on the Wharton Tract in the heart of the Pinelands. The store is said to predate the original section of the ironmaster's mansion, making it the oldest surviving building in the village. It was constructed toward the end of the eighteenth century, following the return of William Richards as furnace manager, three months after the end of the Revolutionary War.

The lower level housed the store itself and the second floor served as a storage warehouse. A company office occupied the upper floors of a brick addition. The main room was whitewashed over roughly plastered walls, the woodwork was painted black, and a stove utilized the chimney west of the many shelves and the counter.

A large variety of merchandise was available. Batsto account books for 1810 and 1814 list fabrics and clothing, china, tableware, items of food, furniture, tools and harnesses.

Atsion Iron Works and later the paper mill at Atsion Lake in Shamong Township, Burlington County, also had a large company store. It adjoined the ironmaster's house built by Samuel Richards in 1826. Both structures have undergone restoration by the New Jersey Bureau of Parks and Forestry.

All the larger glass plants of the area had company-

This elaborate manor house was built by Thomas Richards, Jr., of Atco, in the 1850s. Thomas was the grandson of William Richards, who built the Batsto mansion, and the nephew of Samuel Richards, who built the manor at Atsion.

run stores in which company money was acceptable. The Whitney Glass Works of Glassboro issued five and ten cent paper money, and a brass penny in 1869.

The Whitney Company store ledger gives an example of prices paid by factory hands at about that time:

Molasses	38¢ a gallon
Butter	17¢ a pound
Candles	13¢ a pound
Salt	3¢ a quart
Plug tobacco	2¢ a plug
Eggs	37½¢ a dozen
Coffee	12½¢ a pound
Cranberries	6½¢ a quart

This ledger also contains items written against certain accounts, such as: "Luke Magluke's wife sick. . . . doctor there twice today," and "The Smith family moved. . . . took four window glass."

This way of life, along with the iron, glass and paper factories of the Pines, has long since disappeared. But there are enough reminders that friend Tennessee Ernie was right. You could owe your soul to the company store.

The Circuit Riders

The old Methodist meeting house at Pleasant Mills, still standing, was once a favorite stopping place of itinerant preachers roaming the Jersey woodlands. They could always be sure of an attentive audience and a good, warm meal at the nearby Richards mansion of Batsto.

One day, one of these circuit riders, as they were called, alighted from his sorry looking horse, a much worn Bible under his arm. Hoping to attract attention of the few who happened to be in the vicinity, he called aloud:

"Does anyone here enjoy religion?"

After a moment of silence an old charcoal-burner replied: "Them's that got it do!"

In spite of the many wild tales told through the years by the sensation writers of the tabloids, a great percentage of the Pines people were basically hard working, hard drinking, hard fighting and firm in their beliefs in God, heaven and hell.

As a result, there were established in the Pines such Methodist strongholds as Batsto-Pleasant Mills, Head-of-the-River, Weymouth, and Union Chapel, Port Republic.

The Irish Catholic workmen of the iron furnaces were responsible for the establishment of the log cabin St. Mary's in the Pines, at Sweetwater, and its predecessor Shane's Castle, in the woods of Gloucester County, near Waterford Works.

The Quakers rode many a lonely Pineland mile to a quarterly meeting at Tuckerton or Cape May, until the establishment of the first Quaker meeting house (1774) on the road to Leeds Point.

Preachers riding the old Indian trails were self-sufficient and dedicated. They slept in the open much of the time under horse blankets, and preached wherever they could find a clearing and a gathering of people. As in all human

The Batsto-Pleasant Mills Methodist Church and graveyard.

nature, there were the good and the bad, those who spent their lives on a mission in which they deeply believed, and the others who were looking for no more than a handout and whatever else they could lay their hands on before suddenly departing into the wilds from which they had emerged. But good or bad, they all left their marks.

Religious revivals were an important happening in the Pines, primitive as some may have been. To most of the early inhabitants religion was an emotional experience, many times more emotional than religious. Because of the rugged life led by these people, they needed the promise of a better world elsewhere. Funerals were always dress-up occasions to speed the departed to a more abundant life in the hereafter.

When a log church or meeting house was available, the traveling preacher would make use of it, if the local wardens would let him; otherwise he improvised. Such was the case of the Batsto-Pleasant Mills church.

Dr. Charles Pitman (for whom Pitman was named) was famed for his two-and-a-half-hour sermons. He found the little log cabin church inadequate for the needs of the large crowds he attracted, and used a hay wagon drawn up outside for his pulpit. The wagon was supplied by Jesse Richards, operator of the Batsto Iron Furnace, who was usually host to the man of the Bible, no matter what his religious affiliation, following services.

Although the Batsto church seems today off the beaten track, it attracted a number of well-known preachers of early Jersey days. John Brainerd who, like his brother David before him, devoted his life to the conversion of the Lenni Lenape to Christianity, preached at this spot in 1774. It is recorded that a group of Indians were among his listeners.

The log cabin church was built in 1763 by Captain Elijah

Clark, prominent land owner and later privateer of the American Revolution. It was known as Clark's Meeting House. Rev. Philip Fithian, a Presbyterian minister who was one of the "Indians" in the famous Greenwich tea burning party of the Revolution, mentions in his journal having preached at "Clark's Log Meeting House."

The present church replaced the log one in 1808 and was dedicated by the Rev. Francis Asbury, first Methodist bishop of the United States.

In the cemetery adjoining the church is buried one of its most colorful trustees, Simon Lucas, who occupied that post along with William Richards and Jesse Richards of the Batsto iron family. Simon was known not only for his hell and brimstone interpretation of the Bible, but for bending the rules when the occasion warranted it.

Old-time historian of Sweetwater, Charles F. Green, who would drop into the office of the *Egg Harbor Tribune* in Egg Harbor City on an afternoon to sit and chat, told me a typical Lucas tale as I took notes. I'll attempt to tell it as Green told it to me.

"Old Simon Lucas," said Green, "was a contrary cuss. He could be very much a tyrant with his congregation, as illustrated by his words from the pulpit when a young lady's brooch pin offended him. He denounced her so forcibly she left the church in tears.

"On another occasion he bent a bit. Every spring the Atsion creek would be the scene of a large run of herring. Everyone went after the fish, even to the extent of closing down the iron furnaces. Well, on this Sunday there was an unusually heavy run of herring and the male population of the area turned out with hooks and lines.

"Jesse Richards, of the Batsto works, and his daughter passed by the creek on their way to church. The young miss, shocked at the scene on the Sabbath, said, 'Father, you should stop those men from fishing!'

"Richards replied, 'Don't know if I have the right, but I'll ask Simon Lucas. He should know.'

"On the way back from church, Richards' daughter inquired: 'Papa, did you ask Mr. Lucas about the fishing?'

"'Yes,' answered her father.

"'What did he say?'

"'Well, he said the time to catch herring was when the herring was here!'"

Lightnin' in the Pines

Bog iron workers of the Pines were mostly Irish, Scots, Swedes, Finns and Germans, all hard-working and hard-drinking people. Pineland isolation did not change old habits as the account books of Batsto, Weymouth, Atsion and Martha furnaces indicate.

In the Martha Furnace daily records for 1809 can be found repetitions of this line: "Furnace Blew (went out) at 8 p.m. All Hands Drunk."

And:

July 28—All hands went to the beach.

July 30—All hands returned from the beach—some VERY drunk!

From the Weymouth Furnace diary of 1813:

July 11—Grant and R. Johnson drinking at Steelman's (a tavern) fell in creek.

Aug. 8—Miss Woolfield beat Dan Beaty with broomstick as he was taken to hard drinking.

Aug. 14—W. J. McCurdy, Dan Tremble and Dan Beaty all went to drink down the town. Richard Dempsey laying very drunk by the roadside below Deep Run.

The brew in most cases was Southern Jersey's historic "Lightnin'," allegedly born in the Pines. This was a powerful concoction that for pure wallop made Kentucky Mountain Dew seem mild by comparison.

There were many taverns scattered along the dusty stage routes of the Pines. They were often used for voting places, courts and public meetings, depending on size and location. Bodine's Tavern was a favorite with the Martha Furnace men. It was a few miles south of Martha on the Wading River and known as a "jug tavern."

Now there seem to be several explanations for this title.

One is that a jug tavern was a place where travelers on horseback stopped to fill a saddle bottle or jug. The other and more than likely correct one is that in·these taverns, no matter what drink you ordered, it came from the same jug.

Since most of those who worked in the iron forges and glass factories had no reading ability, the color of a bottle indicated its contents. The shape of the bottle also told the price of the drink. A long-necked one, for instance, could be the lowest priced liquor in the place, and the fat round-shaped one the more costly. To use a current expression of a TV comic, "What you see is what you get." No-one could accuse the tavern keeper of overcharging.

Beer (when available) was sold by the English method of pints and quarts, and an old British custom of marking a customer's consumption was used. A slate was kept for each person seated at a table, especially in places which also provided food, on which was written two letters, "P" for pint and "Q" for quart. Tavern owners were constantly reminding their help to "watch your P's and Q's," which created, according to language scholars, a common expression of today.

A favorite cold weather drink in the Pines was a Stewed Quaker. This consisted of cider with cider oil in it, and a hot roasted apple floating on top. (Cider oil was the oily, spirituous part remaining after the cider was frozen.) The origin of the name is clouded.

Cider with a hot poker from the inn's fireplace thrust into it was also a favorite of the cold months. At stagecoach stops along the Long-a-Coming route from present-day Haddonfield and Berlin to Batsto and Leeds (Leeds Point), passengers were greeted in winter weather by the tavern host with hot rum or mulled cider as they alighted from what was usually a freezing journey.

A drink favored by the Scots and some of the Irish of the

bog forges was "The Scotchem," consisting of applejack, boiling water and a good dash of ground mustard. This concoction, according to reports apparently well-founded, brought tears to the eyes of the drinker, tears that had naught to do with grief.

But Jersey Lightnin' was the native and favorite of the Pines. This was a brew known in other parts of the East, especially apple-growing regions, as applejack, a brandy made from apples by partly freezing hard cider and removing the ice, or by distilling hard cider or fermented apple pomace. The International Encyclopedia defines it as a brew "at one time extensively produced in New Jersey and on account of its ardent and intoxicating qualities known as 'Jersey Lightnin'."

One of the stories told about this Piney drink concerns a city visitor who drove down to the vicinity of Harrisville in search of a sample.

Approaching a man at the side of the road who appeared to be a native, he asked where he could purchase a bottle or two of Jersey Lightnin'.

The native replied, "We got two kinds. What kind you want?"

"Well, I don't know," said the thirsty visitor. "Must I choose?"

"Yep," came the answer, "'cause it depends."

"Depends on what?"

"Depends on whether you're goin' courtin' or fightin'."

Jersey Lightnin' was also used extensively for medicinal purposes, or at least that's what some of the Pinelanders tried to convince me. If used in the proper way, they swore, it was guaranteed to cure colds, flu, snake bites, horse kicks and rheumatism.

The procedure, I was solemnly assured, was to put the patient to bed and cover him with blankets—all but one foot. On this foot was placed a hat. The patient was then given a jug of Jersey Lightnin' and told to drink, and at the same time watch the foot with the hat. When he saw *two* hats, he was cured!

On election day, the Pines taverns, especially those near bog iron or glass furnaces, were exciting places. Candidates who bought the most drinks usually won and the day terminated when no-one was left on his feet to drink or fight.

Workers at furnaces took off on election day. It was an excuse to escape the dull existence of their 6 a.m. to 6 p.m. daily work schedule, seven days a week.

There seems to have been no real attempt by bosses to restrict them. Ironmasters hoped the men would somehow return before the furnaces became too cool and had to be completely refired, a long and costly procedure.

A story is told of election day activities at the old Smith Hotel-Inn, a stagecoach stop on Shore Road, Galloway Township, that is said to have added a new phrase to American political vocabularies.

When Galloway was incorporated in 1789, the Smith Hotel (the Smithville Inn of today) was designated as the official polling place of the township. This meant considerable activity around the hotel-inn as eligible (and some ineligible) voters drove their teams in from surrounding farms and villages to hear candidates, discuss farm crops, cast votes and do a bit of day-off drinking. According to custom, most of the voters would stay around until the polls closed and the ballots were counted. During this time there would be considerable debating and not infrequently the discussions would heat up to the stage of physical combat.

Soon fists would fly, then an occasional jug of spirits. These flying objects did not always reach the mark intended. Some smashed through the inn windows or splattered against its walls. Irate voters, especially those who had been accustomed to shillelaghs back home, would tear boards from the inn, cut tree limbs, and join in the wholesale Donneybrook. By evening there would be quite a few cracked heads.

The desperate innkeeper pleaded with township officers to halt this annual destruction and they responded by ordering a fence erected down the middle of the inn grounds. Whigs and Democrats were assigned their respective sides, and a force of constables, appropriately armed, saw to it that they did no fence hopping. If anyone insisted on settling political differences physically in the nearby woods, but off inn grounds, no one interfered.

The fencing was pulled up after each election and stored by the township until the following year. Then, just before the next polling day, the township's head constable would gather his men and say, "Well, boys, its time to mend our political fences."

The saying became popular and spread. Politicians began using it as a meaning for renewal of acquaintance with their constituents. Thus another colorful South Jersey phrase was added to the language, or so the story goes.

Some sources have credited the phrase to a Senator John Sherman of Ohio (1823–1900), who is said to have declared on one occasion "I have come home to look after my fences," but the South Jerseymen prefer their own version.

They Shall Not Pass!

South Jersey had its own version of the shot heard 'round the world—or at least 'round the Pine Barrens.

Mays Landing, once a shipbuilding center and port of entry at the headwaters of the Great Egg Harbor River, was a favorite Saturday night haunt of the Piney charcoal burners. The "coal bugs," as they were called by the natives, would deliver their week's output of charcoal to the docks and collect their pay, always in cash. With money in pocket, the next move was to get roaring drunk and go on a rampage through the town. Most of the God-fearing citizens of Mays Landing boarded up their places on a Saturday night and prayed for Sunday morning.

Then Captain John May, son of George May, for whom Mays Landing was named, returned home from military duty in the War of 1812. He used his training to set up a system of law and order in the community, where the waterfront people and the farmers and shopkeepers were many times at odds. However, the "coal bugs" proved stubbornly resistant to all attempts at controlling their Saturday-night mayhem. The townspeople appealed to Captain May to put an end to the weekly orgy of drinking, fighting and property destruction.

Man of action that he was, the Captain one Saturday morning planted a small cannon on the bridge leading from the woodlands into the town proper. When the charcoal burners approached, some already far into their celebrating, he threatened to blow them to pieces unless they surrendered all sticks, clubs and firearms, and headed back to the Pines.

Captain May must have been a convincing figure standing there in his army uniform, with a lighted torch, ready to apply it to the cannon charge. There was a hurried consultation among the coalies, who reluctantly threw

71

down their weapons and headed into the Pines from which they had come.

That was the last Mays Landing saw of the burners, and Captain May was the town hero.

Note: We owe a debt to the late Reverend Joel Gilfilan, who put together this story for a celebration marking the fifty-eighth anniversary of the First Presbyterian Church of Mays Landing. The church, the corner-stone of which was laid in April, 1841, has been proposed for the National Registry of Historic Churches.

Look to the Pots

Life for a housewife in the South Jersey Pines during the early 1800s was never easy. There was a constant fear of shortages, especially when the winter snows arrived and there were no nearby stores to supply needs. Even the itinerant peddlers dropped their routes once the icy blasts arrived and roads closed to their box-like wagons.

The Pines farm housewife had to possess a number of skills not necessary for survival today. She knew how to skin and cut up a rabbit or squirrel, how to make sausage links after a pig sticking, how to churn butter and, perhaps most important, how to use a shotgun or rifle to ward off an intruder, animal or otherwise. Above all, she had to see that nothing was wasted.

A small pamphlet published by a Boston company and circulated in the Pines around 1836, attempted to aid the struggling housewife with some common sense advice on everyday living. A well-thumbed and blurred copy of this tract was discovered by the late Mrs. Ethel Noyes, history and antique buff who, together with husband Fred, re-created the South Jersey farm village of Smithville. Dedicated to the housewife who "is not ashamed of economy," the booklet advised:

> "Look frequently to the pails to see that nothing is thrown to the pigs which should have been in the grease-pot.

> "Look frequently to the grease-pot to see nothing is there that might have been served to nourish your own family.

> "See that pork and beef are always under brine and that the brine is sweet and clean. Examine

preserves to see they are not mouldy and pickles that they are not growing soft and tasteless."

Apparently there was quite a bit of carelessness about towels and spoons as the pamphlet warns:

"Count towels, sheets, spoons often as those who use them may have become careless . . . (and thrown them out)."

Confirming the old adage of "waste nothing," the Pines farmwife is told:

"Have bits of bread eaten before they become hard; spread out those not eaten and let them dry to be pounded for puddings or soaked for brewis." (Brewis, a favorite dish of the area, was made from crusts, soaked in hot milk, mashed up and buttered like toast).

"Ox Gall," (it was explained), "will set any color in cotton or woolens. When one lives near a slaughter-house it is worth while to buy cheap, fading, goods and set them with gall which can be purchased for a few cents."

Because a husband was away from the house for long periods, perhaps days, in the pursuit of his work, the young bride got an early lesson in the handling of firearms from her father. She was expected to thus protect her home and, later, children against any roaming Pine robber or chicken-stealing fox. It is reported that many became excellent shots.

Later, when country stores began to spring up at such

places as Chatsworth, Weymouth, Hammonton and Green Bank, there were weekly visits for stocking the cupboard against future needs. The trip was usually made in the flat-bed, springless wagon that served many purposes on a Pineland farm. Besides its importance in the purchasing of necessities, the weekly shopping trip offered a chance to engage in small talk with other farmwives, swap recipes and catch up on all the local area news. It was a major social occasion for women and children alike, many of whom spent the rest of the week in isolation.

The Sunday church service also proved as much a social event as a religious one for country wives, which is why going to services was often made an all-day affair.

Pineland Smugglers
Launch an Industry

To evade customs at the ports of Philadelphia, Greenwich, Toms River, Burlington and Perth Amboy, smugglers would transport their goods across the sandy roads of the Pinelands in flat-wagons, securely hidden under large loads of salt hay. Thus many an illegal cargo escaped detection by roaming customs officials.

Once the goods were delivered to buyers, the salt hay was no longer of use to the smugglers, who promptly dumped it. Enterprising shopkeepers found other uses for the hay, leading to the eventual beginning of salt hay farming as a legitimate enterprise along the Jersey coastlands. Salt hay farming today continues in several coastal spots.

One of the earliest references to salt hay meadows was made in 1685 by Thomas Budd, who owned much of the Pines. He stated that he believed the meadows off the Barrens were excellent grazing lands for cattle because "of the abundance of salt grass." This contention was supported by pioneer farmers of Cape May, Ocean and Atlantic Counties, who swam their cattle across small stretches of water separating the mainland from the off-shore islands (or used raft-like barges where the water was deep) and allowed them to roam free. Although this land was officially owned by the Jersey Proprietors, farmers ignored the jurisdiction.

However, it was the activities of the smugglers which started a demand for salt meadow hay and farmers, who previously had cut some at various times for bedding of their horses, began to see its commercial value.

They constructed makeshift landings on the mainland and ferried the hay across the meadows in flat scows. The best of the salt meadows yielded as much as three tons to

76

the acre, from two cuttings per season. Although there
was a total of seventy-four statutes on the books of
New Jersey between 1697 and 1783 regulating the use of
meadowlands, those involved in the new possibilities of salt
grass paid little heed to them.

When the first glass factories began operation in the
deep Pines along the Mullica River, there was a big demand
for salt hay for the packing of glassware and pottery.
Rough roads pocked with tree stumps were the only lanes
of communication between the Pinelands and the markets
of Philadelphia and New York, and the shipment of glass
over these roads was a decided risk. Therefore the early
glass houses of the Pines depended upon the currents of
the Mullica.

Glass was packed at such landings as Hermann City,
Crowleytown, and Bulltown, and shipped by water to waiting merchants in the two large urban centers. The demand
for packing grass accelerated with the demand for glassware. Then banana firms in Newark and New York City
began using salt hay as packing for banana shipments,
creating one of the first markets out of the Southern Jersey
territory.

Ice houses in the vicinity found salt hay of particular
benefit as insulation, and many times sent their own people
to gather the grass, which proved a cheap means of keeping ice stocks during the warmer months. However, this
system did not prove profitable, and soon the ice houses
were customers of farmers who began to spend more of
their time on the salt meadows. Some eventually became
known as salt hay farmers who gained their entire liveli-
hood from the business.

The paper mill at Harrisville used salt hay in the making
of so-called "butcher paper," a course brown paper used
primarily by butchers for the wrapping of their meats back

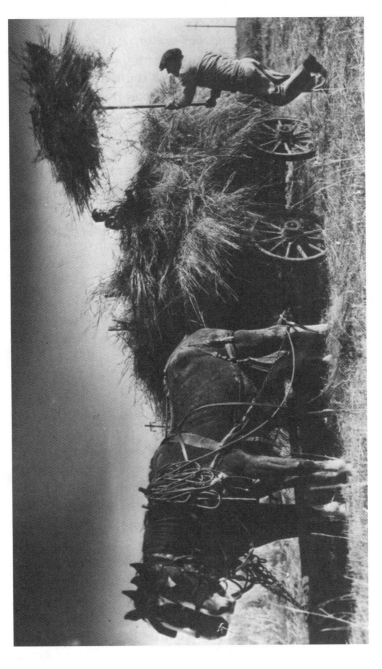

Rare old photo of salt hay gathering on the meadows of South Jersey, an industry launched by the needs of smugglers.

in the days before modern sanitary restrictions. William
McCarthy, who bought the mill in 1832, found a ready
supply of salt hay in the Wading River area. According to
mill records, it was turning out nearly a ton of paper daily
by 1835. McCarthy's hay was brought by barges to the
Landing (Lower Bank, Burlington County) about a mile
below the mill and conveyed from there by mule team. Salt
hay farmers were getting three dollars per ton for their
efforts. The usual Mullica River barge was of twenty
ton capacity.

Many of the flat-decked craft of the Mullica, commonly
called hay scows, existed up to about 1935. The scow varied
in size, the most common being thirty-three feet long and
about twelve feet wide. They drew very little water even
when fully loaded. This made them perfect for the shallow
Mullica and its tributaries. There are still some to be seen
pulled up on the mud banks of the river, now rotting hulks,
victims of time, storm and tide.

The Colorful Webers

Most salt hay farmers found enough work to keep them busy throughout the year. When not actually cutting and hauling hay, they were repairing their equipment or tending growing vegetable crops of their own. Necessity forced them to have many skills, including ship building and blacksmithing.

Individuals had their own methods of salt grass farming. Some used teams, some an Indian sling (two poles on which hay was tied and then carried to their craft—a trick learned from the Lenni Lenape Indians), while others had oxen to carry, or rather drag, the load. No matter which method was used, it was back-breaking work.

Charlie Weber was the king of the salt hay men in the vicinity of Wading River and the Mullica. Dr. Henry C. Beck in his *Jersey Genesis* gives a lot of first hand information about Charlie and his hay business, having been fortunate enough to have talked with him on the subject. That, however, was a bit before my time of jotting down South Jersey lore, and I missed talking to the colorful Charlie himself. But I was able to spend an interesting afternoon with his daughter, Mrs. Emilie (Weber) Brown, and her husband at the Brown farm in Wading River.

Emilie Weber Brown, daughter of the legendary Charlie Weber, hayman of the Mullica, and her husband.

Emilie, a Weber every bit as colorful as her dad, shared his work and hardships like "one of the boys," as she expressed it. She confirmed that hay gathering was a rough, tough job, but her father persisted in carrying out his work to the end of his years (he was seventy-five when he died). He spurned the urgings of his sons to take life easier and give up the hay business entirely. But Weber did make one concession to sons Ed and Charlie, Jr., Emilie recalled. He installed a "dang-fangled put-put" (gas motor) on the back of his scow, doing away with the necessity for the long pole-oars which he used for many years to get his loaded barge upstream.

The original Weber farm was at Weekstown, about four miles from Lower Bank on the Old Gloucester County (now Atlantic County) side of the Mullica, deep within the Pinelands. It was there when Charlie's father, a grain merchant, arrived from Germany with his wife and two small children. Like so many other Germans who settled in the Barrens, Weber came to this country to escape the constant wars among the German states and the ever-present threat of conscription. The farm consisted of one big barn, a number of small storage buildings and a modest farmhouse. These out-structures were used by Charlie Weber to stable his horses and store hay awaiting a pickup by buyers.

The town or hamlet was called Weeksville because so many of the Weeks family settled there; they are still the most prominent name in the place today, now known as Weekstown. All the Weber children went to school in a one-room schoolhouse at Weekstown, according to Emilie.

Charlie Weber, born in 1869, was only seventeen years old when he bought the farmstead and went into the salt hay business in a big way. A few years after he started he was harvesting 500 tons of hay from the Wading River meadowland, Mrs. Brown recalled, as she poured another cup of hot coffee and set it upon the linoleum covered kitchen table.

According to Mrs. Brown, all kinds of flat barges were pressed into service. These were rowed up and down the river as the tides demanded. Many times Emilie herself took a turn at the big pulling oar, which was about twenty feet long. There would be one rower to each side of the barge. This balanced it. Mrs. Brown said that most times her uncle would take one side and her father the other. They knew the river and its currents and used them to full advantage. But there was still a lot of rowing to be done.

The Weber barges docked at The Landing and the hay was tossed off and stacked. One particular craft had a small cabin which contained an iron cook stove, a table, some boxes which served as chairs, and closets in which food was stored. During cutting season everyone was about before daybreak, and the barge was well on its way downstream by the time the sun was peeping over the meadows. They would try to return by nightfall. This was not always possible according to Emilie. Many times the hay crew would sleep on the meadows.

Having had personal experience with the greenhead flies and mosquitoes which swarm over a meadow, I was curious to discover how it was possible to stay overnight without the aid of modern lotions, sleeping bags, nettings and other protective equipment. "They (the skeeters) would be a bother, yes," said Mrs. Brown, "but one got toughened to them. You kept as near the fire as possible." When horses were along they would be completely covered by a special burlap blanket. She then added, "It is a known fact that a Jersey mosquito will not bother a real down Jerseyman—his hide is too tough!"

I could not but feel that here was another bit of famous

Salt hay wagons mired in the meadows at the tip of the Pine Barrens in Ocean County.

South Jersey folk talk, since several cranberry growers had already told me the same tale.

Mrs. Brown confirmed that Harrisville's paper mill used salt hay, and recalled that her father took a lot of his harvest to Harrisville and sold it there. Salt hay was bringing from $10 to $12.50 per ton in those times, she said. Weber did not own all the land he cut. Some was rented, some "just borrowed." This seems to be the story with many other salt hay men of the times.

Emilie also explained drying, another part of the operation. An agreed cutting of salt hay was made and left to dry. It was loaded onto the scow about a week later. In this way there was always a bargeload of hay ready for market.

While Mr. and Mrs. Brown may well by Pineys in the modern sense of the word, they consider themselves "bay people," part of a fast vanishing race of seashore natives. Although the active salt hay days are gone, there are a lot of memories floating around the Brown homestead. I reluctantly turned my car onto a sandy road and waved goodbye to a cheery "come back soon."

You Gotta Have Bounce

No, this title does not refer to a new dance step; it concerns one of the principal crops of the Pine Barrens. Cranberries were known as "sasemineash" to the Lenni Lenape Indians and later as "crane-berries" to the early Pine settlers, because of the crane-like formation of its flower. They grew wild in the marshlands of Ocean, Burlington, Atlantic and some parts of Gloucester counties.

In the middle 1800s cranberry men began to take over large parts of this great marsh and put scientific and business know-how into the growing and marketing of the berries. They also created such unusual place names as Hog Wallow, Double Trouble, Penny Pot, Mt. Misery and Friendship.

One of the most colorful characters in early cranberry culture was Peg Leg John Webb of Cassville, a one-legged Ocean county schoolmaster who discovered that healthy berries had to have bounce and invented a simple way of testing them—a wooden stairway.

Peg Leg would take his baskets of freshly scooped cranberries from his bogs and roll them down a flight of steps. If they bounced from step to step with a certain zip he knew they were good. Those that did not bounce were discarded.

According to present-day county agricultural agents, this theory was perfectly sound and it is still used for sorting cranberries. However, the crude steps have been replaced by more scientific machinery.

Old Peg Leg Webb had a good market for his berries on the Philadelphia waterfront docks, where he received $50 a barrel for them, a large sum of money for the times. His heaviest buyers were whaling ship captains leaving American shores for long periods of time. They had found that cranberries would prevent the disease of scurvy, which attacked every crew in the days of sail.

Before the advent of machine picking, cranberries were picked with wooden scoops that "combed" the berries from the plants. Here is a typical harvesting scene, with handscooping being done in overlapping rows. (*Courtesy of Ocean Spray Cranberries, Inc.*)

South Jersey was producing half of all American cranberries by 1870, with the pine bogs of Burlington County
the most productive, as they are today.

Thanks to another schoolmaster, Andrew Rider of
Hammonton, founder of Rider College in Trenton, the
South Jersey berries were introduced to the royal courts of
Europe. Royal favor led to the opening of a large foreign
market and Rider finally quit the scholarly life to cultivate
and promote cranberries full time. He even entered a
horse by the name of Cranberry in the English Derby—
and won!

Working the cranberry bogs provided yearly fall jobs
for most of the original Pineys. The first berries were
harvested by workers wading knee-deep in the bogs, armed
with wooden scoops. Today the berries are gathered by
machines and scientific know-how. But they still get bounced.

Moving Day

South Jersey's first farmers were far less scientific than their brothers of today. They knew nothing of crop rotation, balanced fertilizers, or irrigation, and did most of their planting by instinct and tradition rather than book calculation. They were sucessful to a degree, but they overworked the land to the point where it became useless for further crops. Not knowing any remedy for revitalization of this land, the farmers' solution was usually to pack up and move to other fields more promising.

This led to a now forgotten South Jersey institution—Moving Day—which was March 25. There were two main reasons for choosing this date. One was the fact that it was about the time that spring work begins on the farm; the other was that in earlier times (according to the old Roman calendar of Julius Caesar) March 25 was New Year's Day. It was approximately the time of the vernal equinox and the thawing of frozen ground.

Moving Day in the 1800s was a gala time, in spite of the hard work involved. Farmers helped one another in the moving process and when it had finally become accomplished, there was a feast in which everyone joined.

Moving a farm family required serveral teams of horses. These always seemed available, as were the many hands needed to move heavy furniture. Dishes had to be packed in barrels, and mirrors and wall pictures were wrapped in old quilts, to prevent breakage when they were loaded onto the springless farm wagons for the journey over bumpy roads to their new destination.

Oil lamps were carried on someone's lap in the front seat of the wagon. Despite this care, a move many times resulted in a certain amount of damage to household articles. Some farm families were moving every couple of years, to plots in the same neighborhood, while others found their way clear across the state to another South Jersey county. The Benjamin Franklin comment, "Three removes are as bad as a fire," suggests that moving days were a bit of a problem even back in his era.

Moving Day volunteers were divided into two sets of helpers. One group would assist the family in removing the furniture from the house and the tools from the barn; the other would be on hand to set things up at the new location. Much time was spent by the women in cleaning the old farmhouse before it was closed to await the next tenant. This was a practice followed religiously by farm wives.

Once the work was completed there was a dinner. The womenfolk pitched in and cooked, served and washed dishes. Chicken pot pie was the most popular dish for such an occasion, complete with vegetables, relishes, cakes, pies and puddings. Those engaged in helping with the moving process brought their own offerings to the feast. Sometimes there would be a dozen kinds of pie and no end of layer cakes, cookies, buns and preserved fruits. No store boughten goods for the farmers of South Jersey!

Later-day house warming rituals may well have stemmed from these festivities centered around old South Jersey's Moving Day.

Cure Thyself—Pines Style

Physicians, competent or otherwise, were few and far between in the Pine Barrens of yesterday. Dr. James Still of Medford-Indian Mills, the "Black Doctor of the Pines," was an exception and he had never formally studied medicine. For the most part the woodland people cared for their own ills and hurts by using time-tried remedies, many handed down from the Indians, others brought from Europe by new settlers. Most would cause horror, or wry amusement, among doctors today. However, according to the stories handed down to us, these cures worked. If they didn't, there are no survivors left to say so.

Some of the old customs still endure—mud and spit for a bee or wasp sting, for example. You take a bit of dirt from the soil upon which you are standing, spit on it to moisten, and rub the mixture on the stinging area. It works. I know, because I have used this basic treatment many times myself, out in the woods.

Other cures are not so simple. Dr. Still himself had quite a few down-to-earth remedies recorded in his autobiography, first printed in 1877 and reprinted by the Medford Historical Society in 1971. Among them was this treatment for fever:

"I ordered my patient to bathe all over with soda-water or weak lye, the whole surface to be rubbed with it. Next sudorific medicine followed with warm catnip tea. If the head is hot take whiskey, vinegar and soft water, one teacup of each and one teaspoon of fine salt; mix and apply cold several times a day. . ."

Here are a few other home remedies gathered from various sources among the old timers of the region:

Earache: Soak feet in warm water; or roast an onion and put the heart of it into the ear as warm as can be borne; or heat a brick and wrap it up and apply to side of head. Cotton wool, wet with sweet oil is also good.

Chills and Fever: Drape patient tightly in a sheet and run him around the house three times. Jump *under* the bed. The latter allows the chill or fever to jump *onto* the bed. Keep this up until they are gone or the patient falls exhausted. If the activity does not kill the patient it will cure the chill.

For Colds: Take oil made from the fat of a skunk and rub it on the chest. This is no way to win friends but it may shock the cold from the system. Another remedy is a drop of turpentine on the tongue daily. Also, eating garlic keeps a cold, and neighbors, away. A proven remedy is to soak both feet in a tub of hot water and sip away at Port wine. It may not necessarily cure the cold, but it puts the patient in a much improved state of mind.

Many old-timers kept a bottle of Jersey Lightnin' or just plain old rye whiskey handy for colds, snakebite, or whatever excuse they could muster up.

To Stop Sneezing: Look at the tip of your nose with both eyes at the same time.

For Boils, Blisters and Burns: Have someone chew a plug of tobacco and spit the juice on the sore spots.

For Dyspepsia: Mix one gallon of hickory ashes and one gallon of water. Let it stand for two or three days in the chimney corner, stirring occasionally. Strain off, first adding a wine glass of soot. Take one half teaspoon a half hour after each meal.

For Quincy: Bathe the neck with bear grease and pour it down the throat. Goose grease is a good substitute if there are no bears available.

For Fevers: The use of malt beer is a good preservative against fevers. Bottoms up!

Food Poisoning: A teaspoon of vinegar in a glass of water every five minutes is guaranteed to either cure you or make you sicker than you are.

Extracting Corns: Cut a raw cranberry in half and put the cut side to the foot. This will ease out the corn.

To Cure Wakefulness: The Pines pioneers generally had no need of the great array of products advertised on TV today to induce sleep. But if, after working hard from dawn to dusk, one still needed something to make him drowsy, he tried a mixture of vinegar and honey, a teaspoon of which taken before going to bed insured pleasant dreams.

Stomach Disorders: Take a spoonful of ashes and stir it in cider, then drink. Even some Piney medics favored this.

For Canker: Hold some burnt alum in the mouth. Tea made from wild violets is also good. Every family should gather violets for this purpose.

For Sore Throat: Cover a slice of salt pork with red pepper, and bind to throat before going to bed. Or take stocking off foot and bind around neck while it is still warm.

Berries are good for a number of medical situations. Blackberries are useful in case of dysentery. Whortleberries (huckleberries) dried are a useful medicine for children. Made into tea and sweetened with molasses, they are good for relief of restrictions. All berries have health powers.

The careful farm or woods family always kept kerosene and turpentine handy for a variety of medical purposes. Kerosene will take the poison out of a snake bite; it is a good disinfectant. Turpentine kills infection in a cut and starts the healing process. It is also good to thin out paint.

Whiskey poured onto a wound prevents infection. Pour some inside first to withstand the burn of the outside application.

The Pineys were and are a hearty bunch!

The Fascination of Ongs Hat

Ongs Hat is a dot on a road map smack in the center of
the deep Pines of Burlington County, somewhere midway
between the crossroads of Buddtown and Mt. Misery on
Route 70.

Here the story should end, but it doesn't, because this
odd little dot on the map has a strange fascination which
has sent newswriters and others tramping about the under-
brush for years trying to pinpoint its location and provide
answers about its elusive history.

Meanwhile, stories and legends about the name of Ongs
Hat gain with each new year and each new exploration,
furnishing argument for many a wintertime gathering
around a log fire.

Ongs Hat or its legend apparently came into being some
time in the 1800s. The first account of Ongs Hat I came
across related how a Mr. Ong, quite a dandy of the Pines,
was making too many passes at a certain young lady during
the course of a Saturday night get-together, and neglect-
ing the spirited miss he had brought to the affair. After
delivering herself of a few hot words, said young miss
grabbed his prized hat, ran to the bank of a nearby stream
and flung it onto a limb overhanging the water.

Ong was unable to recover it, and so the hat stayed there
indefinitely. Everyone began calling the place Ongs Hat,
for want of a better name. What happened to Mr. Ong, the
hat tosser, or the hat itself, no one seems to know.

However, a Pines character I chanced to meet up there a
few years back said this story is just not true. What really
happened, according to his version, as told to him by a
friend, who claimed acquaintance with Mr. Ong, is that the
latter had a slight partiality for Jersey Lightnin'. On his
way home from one all-night affair, the exuberant Mr.
Ong tossed his hat in the air. It caught on a tree limb

overhanging a small stream. Mr. Ong evidently felt that
the hat was not worth retrieving and so there it remained.

Shortly after I had included these facts in a newspaper
article, the late Frank Toughill of the *Philadelphia Bulletin*
wrote me that neither story was true. He had talked to
a C. Clinton Zeller, who was chief of Burlington County
detectives and a resident of the area for years. Frank said
Zeller's version was this: Mr. Ong was a Chinese cook for a
Philadelphia merchant's family with whom he was traveling
seaward for the summer. Jersey stages at that time were
rather drafty, and Ong's hat blew off. The merchant
shouted to the stage driver to stop until Ong could retrive
his hat.

The merchant, ever on the lookout for a new business
venture, himself alighted from the stage, looked about,
and decided that the spot, halfway between the Delaware
River and the Atlantic Ocean, was ideal for a stage stop inn.

The inn was built shortly afterward and called Ongs Hat.
It was destroyed some time later by one of the fires that fre-
quently sweep through the Pines. While the inn is long gone,
Frank concluded, the name remains. (A drive-in called
"Ongs Hat" near the spot today carries on the tradition.)

Alfred Jones, a supervising warden for the southern
area of the Pines, had an additional version. There is no
foundation to the Chinese cook story, he contended. "Ong
was an Indian. The way I heard it was this: One day
Indian Ong disappeared. There was evidence he had been
murdered but the body was never found. His bloody hat
was discovered in the brush and the crossroads was soon
referred to in stories of the crime as Ongs Hat."

John W. Haines, who was born in the Barrens, descendant of a family that settled there before the American
Revolution and who now lives in Medford Lakes, disagrees
with the whole cadre of story tellers.

"Ong," he told listeners, "was neither a Chinese or an Indian. He was a Dutchman who lived at Middle-of-the Shore, the early name for Tuckerton. Ong would take his family from Tuckerton to Burlington once a year. It was a two-day trip. This particular time Ong stopped halfway and built a lean-to for the night.

The Dutch name for a lean-to is *hoet,* the same from which the word *hut* is derived. Ong called his lean-to Ong's Hoet. Later it was corrupted to Ongs Hat."

If you want to collect your own version of the origin of Ongs Hat, just ask anyone in the neighborhood. You can be assured of originality, since the Pines people excel as story tellers. They are also known, however, for their knack of embellishing a simple tale.

Ongs Hat is still a dot on a road map, and a mis-punctuated one at that, but the most interesting dot you will ever find.

Historic Note: On the factual side of the Ongs Hat story is evidence that a Jacob Ong, a Quaker, resided in Mansfield Township, Burlington County, in 1699. He purchased, among other parcels, about one hundred acres in the vicinity of what is now known as Ongs Hat. The land was mainly cedar swamp and stunted pine. Whether Ong actually had a shack of some kind at the spot has never been substantiated. Some time later Mr. Ong moved to Pennsylvania and the name disappeared from the records.

There was a tavern near the site in 1800, operated by Issac Haines. The name Ongs Hat is found on a road map of 1828.

The First Dual Highway

The Pines people claim that the first dual highway in the state of New Jersey was not an invention of the automobile generation but existed back in stagecoach days.

It was located at a spot deep in the woodlands between Atsion, Quaker Bridge and Batsto, in what is now known as the Wharton Tract. The dual road was a part of the old stage route from Long-a-Coming to Atsion, Quaker Bridge, Washington and on to Wading River and Tuckerton.

Creation of this road, approximately a mile long, was the result of heavy stagecoach traffic through the Pines just prior to the advent of the iron horse, which put the stages out of business.

The road was originally wide enough for just a single vehicle. At no place between Atsion and Batsto was there enough room for two vehicles to pass. Because of increasing stage traffic, a second roadway was cleared for about a mile.

Stage drivers were aware of schedules of fellow drivers and would time themselves to arrive at the bypass so that the two vehicles could pass without a mishap. In warm weather passengers would alight, stretch cramped muscles, roam about, perhaps heat a few biscuits (journey cakes) and collect flowers, there being no restrictions in those days. At the driver's shrill whistle, they would again pile into the coach and continue the journey.

But you will always find a character who will dispute this practical story. Gullible hikers and seekers of information are confidently told that this second road was cut unexpectedly by a wild team of horses one twilight after Himself, the ole Jersey Devil, suddenly appeared in the middle of the original roadway. That it must have taken a strong team of horses to topple the trees and brush is ignored. After all, why spoil a good story with facts?

The dual highway, however, *is* located in the deepest

part of the Pines, far from human habitation. Should the Pines monster suddenly appear, there is no doubt that the hiker thus confronted would take little note of whether or not his flight followed a legitimate road.

You can still discern its outlines today if you care to do a bit of hiking, say about fourteen miles worth. Start at Batsto, make your way toward Atsion Lake and there you are.

Try the path some Autumn evening, say, within the eve of All Souls Day. It might prove interesting!

Coffin is Buried

The flames of the War of 1812 were still burning when William Coffin arrived at what is now Hammonton, on the edge of the Wharton Tract in the Pines, to conduct a lumber business. He built a sawmill near the lake and operated it there until 1817, when he joined Jonathan Haines in a new glass venture.

Coffin continued his activities until 1836, when he leased his holdings to his son Bodine Coffin and a son-in-law Andrew K. Hay. The locale at that time was known as Coffin's Works or Coffin-Town.

Coffin was also interested in real estate and had large holdings near his mill. When it began to appear that a village would spring up around the spot, and other South Jersey developers such as Richard Brynes and Charles K. Landis (founders of Vineland and Sea Isle City) became interested in the area, it was decided that the name Coffin-ville or Coffintown on their literature was not conducive to sales. Coffin made the decision to erase his name and substitute that of his son, John HAMMOND Coffin, on brochures urging settlement in the new development. So Coffintown became Hammond's Town, later shortened to its present form of Hammonton. One must admit this sounds more inviting.

Hammonton is the only official "town" in South Jersey, as opposed to "borough" or "city."

Matter of a Name

Most scholars agree that the village of Absecon, a former Indian camping ground on the edge of the Pine Barrens in Atlantic County, derives its name from a word in the Lenni Lenape language— "Absegami," meaning "Little Sea Water."

Not necessarily so, according to the late Jake Lingelbach, father of Mrs. Ethel Noyes, who founded and built the sprawling Historic Towne of Smithville on Shore Road.

Jake's version, told to me one afternoon as we sat on the glass enclosed porch of his home in Port Republic, concerned a fisherman of Absecon Creek who was plagued by thefts of his fishing gear.

He finally bought a dog and named him Abner, or "Ab" for short.

Whenever this fisherman found someone near his equipment he would call his dog and cry "Ab-sic-em!"

And that was how the town was named, according to Jake.

The Wrangles of Wrangleboro

Port Republic is a pretty little community nesting sleepily on the edge of the Jersey Pines, secure in its tree lined streets, its general old time air and its historic dwellings dating to the post-Revolutionary period. It is dominated by the tall spire of the Port Republic Methodist Church, built in 1800 and often called the "Christmas Card Church" because of its rustic simplicity of line that is especially picturesque when the winter snows drift around it.

But things were not always this quiet and peaceful in Port Republic. In fact the Port was at one time so boisterous, with six nearby taverns and their clientele of brawling woodsmen, baymen and shipyard workers, that it was known as Wrangleboro. It is certainly true that wrangles were quite frequent. Many heads were bashed and eyes closed. Tossed bottles smashed against the walls and often the free-for-alls spilled out upon the surrounding roads. "Everyone had a fine time until some pious people started demanding law and order," an old bayman once told me nostalgically.

Once a Port Republic lady berated me loudly for telling the Wrangleboro story at a lecture, even after I showed her the original name on some old maps. "Nonsense," she snapped, "it's a printer's mistake." My Wrangleboro informant, after pouring his second shot of Jersey brew (for which I was paying) brooded: "She's the kind that stopped all the fun."

While no exact records seem to have been kept on the inns and their wranglings, the consensus is that at least six existed in the vicinity, including the Franklin Inn (now restored as a private dwelling), the Red Stag, and Smith's Hotel or Baremore Tavern as it was sometimes called, further down Moss Mill Road towards Leeds Point.

"Let's stop messing words," my drinking companion

said. "Historians like to call these places taverns or inns—sounds real poetic. Truth is they were saloons or pubs, nothing more, where a man could drink, let off steam and forget his troubles. There was a bar, a rough wooden one, sometimes a couple of tables and if you went under you stretched out on the floor and the other customers stepped over you. Sometimes they were not too careful and that's when the fighting started."

Most of the heavy drinkers, he said, came from nearby sawmills and shipyards. Others were clammers and fishermen, with a few charcoal burners for good measure. As in the old West, there was usually a running feud between one group and another and it didn't take much to start off a real blaster.

The Franklin Inn, the most historic one of the vicinity, was built about 1750 by Daniel Mathis. It welcomed stage coach travelers and was a regular stop on all routes. One such traveler was the Philadelphia printer Benjamin Franklin. According to historians, he stopped there during trips to Leeds Point to consult with Daniel Leeds, who was publishing almanacs which pre-dated Franklin's own *Poor Richard's Almanac.* It was during one of Franklin's stay-overs that a gay party was held and the inn was formally named in his honor.

Sleeping quarters were cramped, since the original rooms were only nine by five feet. They were on the second floor of the building. Candles were kept in every window to light the way for after-dark travelers. Today, candles (electric ones) still shine in every window, although the place long ago ceased its original pursuits.

Brimstone Hill was also a name for the vicinity, supposed to have been bestowed upon it by a traveling "hell-fire" circuit rider.

Another small settlement grew up around the Red Stag

Inn, including a mill known as "Clark's," which gained its
name from Elijah Clark, who was born there in 1743.
Clark, along with Richard Wescoat, played an important
part in the American Revolution and was among the
privateers of the "nest of rebel pirates" at Chestnut Neck
on the Mullica. The Red Stag, where many of the wrangles
took place, was a favorite with stage coach drivers after a
dusty trip through the Pines. Nothing now remains of the
inn or the mill.

The conversion of Wrangleboro started with the establishment of Union Chapel, the first house of worship in the
community and grand-daddy of the present "Christmas
Card Church." Residents embarrassed by the name
Wrangleboro sought to have it officially changed; after
a town meeting they decided on the name Unionville.
However, postal authorities pointed out that there were
already too many Union-somethings in New Jersey, including Union County, and demanded a new name.

After a second town meeting the community chose to
call itself Port Republic, a thoroughly respectable sounding,
if mystifying, name since the town does not have a port.

Historic Note: Although the town is on Nacote Creek it was never
officially designated a port of entry. Some believe that the "port" was a
tribute to the shipbuilders and the seamen who made the place their
home. Regardless, the Post Office department accepted the name,
everybody was happy, and no one questioned the strict application of
the word.

Swimming Over Point

Tramping one day along the banks of the lower Mullica River, which flows through the Pinelands and separates Burlington and Atlantic Counties, I came to a spot the natives called Swimming Over Point.

I sensed a story and was not disappointed.

It seems that back in the early days of this region there were no bridges over the Mullica, but somehow the old game of boy meets girl flourished among the local Quaker youth, especially those who had become acquainted during Quarterly Meeting at Tuckerton. Mere lack of a bridge was no obstacle to courting.

When a boy from Atlantic County (then Old Gloucester) wanted to visit a girl on the Burlington side of the river, he stripped, packed his clothes on his head, and swam across to the opposite bank, allowing himself time to dry off before continuing his journey.

What happened in winter no one seems to know. Probably all bets were called off until the following spring, since the river is too rapid at this point to freeze.

A river banks character told me that the water was rather shallow there, and at times the older Quakers on way to Meeting would swim their horses across.

There is also at least one instance when an entire wedding party crossed that way. This was before Quakers from both sides got together and built Quaker Bridge, a few miles above Batsto.

The First Drive-in

South Jersey Taverns were important gathering places just prior to and during the Revolutionary War. Here notices were tacked, news disseminated and recruiting campaigns carried on. When stagecoach lines were established, the taverns became terminals.

The first drive-in tavern in the nation may have been the old Stone Tavern of Greenwich, Cumberland County, N.J., on the Lower Road at Bacon's Neck. It was kept by Jacob Ware in the years 1728 and 1729 and from 1741 to 1743, and is usually referred to as the oldest inn of John Fenwick's manor town. Located on a well traveled road in the days when gentlemen doing business between one town and another rode by horse along dusty trails, the tavern was a welcome stopping place.

Such a stop, however, consumed much time, as it entailed watering and feeding the horse by the inn groom while the rider partook of food and drink in the main room, usually occupied by others who were in the mood for leisurely talk. Many of the businessmen, lawyers, and officials who felt the necessity for the stop complained of the loss of hours in the customary proceedings.

Tavern-keeper Ware made his bid for lasting fame when he resolved the problem by cutting a small window in the north wall of the tavern, at a height that a man on horseback could reach as he rode up, be served his ale or rum without dismounting, place his empty glass on a shelf provided, and be off on his business. A convenient water trough and hay were provided for his horse.

It is reported that this arrangement became highly popular, and Ware did a thriving business without realizing that he had created a bit of history by becoming the daddy of the modern drive-in restaurant with its many time-saving devices.

The Mysterious Lost Silver Mine

One of the ghosts of today's Pines is Carmantown, a small village of woodchoppers, charcoal burners and huckleberry pickers on the road to Mays Landing in what was at that time "Old Gloucester" County. Today it is no more than open fields.

This was the home of the Carmans, a German family which eventually became entwined with the Mason family of Absecon Island to create one of the largest family trees of the area. A reunion of both families is held yearly at Lake Lenape, Mays Landing, not far from the original village.

According to Willard Mason Rogers of Sarasota, Florida, one of the historians of the Mason clan, Carmantown was purchased by George Carman, a direct descendant of the original Mark Kurrmann, who came to this country from Germany before the American Revolution and Anglicized his name to Mark Carman.

The land was paid for, according to an old document, with "200 new silver dollars which had been coined from silver ore which George Carman and two others dug from a silver mine they discovered on the Doughty Estate between Pleasantville and Pomona." This is a mystifying and tantalizing statement since to the best of anyone's knowledge there are no significant silver deposits anywhere in the Pine Barrens.

A most diligent search of George Carman's personal correspondence has failed to pinpoint the alleged mine location, nor are there any other references to the secret mine in subsequent family papers. Current descendants are puzzled by the lost mine reference, and are prone to doubt its existence.

According to geologists, a silver mine of any size in the South Jersey woodlands is unlikely. Professor William Parrott, Jr., of Stockton State College, on the fringe of the

Pines, noted a possibility that some silver had at times found its way into the local soil but "never enough to make a profitable mine possible."

A folklore buff has suggested that perhaps the "silver mine" may have been part of a treasure buried long years before by pirates who were known to frequent the Jersey bays and inlets.

One of the few written references to Carmantown is found in the log of an itinerant preacher, the Reverend Albert Matthews, who wrote in 1860: "In this place (Carmantown) our house of worship was a miserable log cabin. All the houses except one were made of logs."

The year 1872 seems to have been the beginning of the end of Carmantown, although the name appeared on maps of 1904. Demand for charcoal had dwindled by then and most of the Carmans moved away, many to Absecon Island and the new Atlantic City where the family received its Mason connection.

Carmantown has long ago joined other ghosts of the Pines, but the "lost mine" is still a popular topic of discussion at Pines gatherings.

Music in the Pines

The natural music of the Pine Barrens is the quiet murmuring of trees at dusk, the croaking of the little green frogs in the nearby ponds and marshes, the calls of the wild birds and the rippling of shimmering streams making their way to the ocean. They merge into a woodlands symphony that is often complex and quite beautiful.

However, there is another kind of native music born in the Pines and preserved by such dedicated groups as the Pinehawkers and the Pineconers, as well as many individual wandering minstrels. All are proud to call themselves Pineys, and they seek to preserve the tunes and musical techniques disappearing all too fast, as time takes its toll of traditional players.

Pineland music centers in the Waretown, Bamber, Forked River district of Ocean County. Whereas New Orleans jazz has Preservation Hall, Pinelands music has had the Homeplace and the present Albert Hall.

The Homeplace was actually the home of legendary Joe Albert who, during the depression years, purchased a fifty-one acre plot at Waretown and built a house to be used principally by his hunting and fishing companions. The latter persuaded him to make it large enough to accommodate music fans for Saturday night gatherings, chipping in on the costs. This soon became known as the Homeplace, the first official hall of Piney music.

The weekly "Saturday Night Jamborees" continued for nineteen years and ended in 1973 when they became so popular that the Homeplace couldn't accommodate them.

Pines musicians were without a home until a year later, when the owner of a market on Route 9 in Waretown agreed to rent a small hall or barn to the rear of his other buildings. Thus the present Albert Hall was born. All concerned will tell you, however, this is only a temporary stop until they can amass enough funds to build a large place to hold the overflow crowds which turn up every Saturday night for the all-night doings.

Joe Albert

The original Pinehawkers consisted of Bill Britton on the fiddle, Merce Ridgway, Sr., on guitar, and Walt Britton on banjo. Walt was a cousin to Bill and brother-in-law to Merce, Sr. Vocalist of the group, according to his widow

Myrtle, was Merce, Sr., who started composing songs soon after they were married forty years ago. (As I write these lines word has just come of Merce's death in July, 1980.)

While Merce, Sr. wrote much of the music, there was one collaboration, a song titled "Home in the Pines." Mrs. Ridgway said that Bill Britton brought the words to her husband and asked if he could put music to them. He did, and the trio featured the number for years. It is strictly South Jersey in flavor.

Besides being friends, neighbors and relatives, the musicians worked together in the charcoal pits and at other occupations in the Ocean County Pines, playing first at informal family gatherings and for friends, according to Merce, Jr., who now leads the current Pinehawkers.

For a brief period, their career extended further afield. In 1941, Dorothea Dix Lawrence, an opera singer, folklorist and author, of Plainfield, N.J., was searching for authentic Pineland music for a national festival in Washington, D.C. Coming to Forked River (that's pronounced Fork-ed, you city folk) she sought advice from postmaster Ralph Penn who said, "Go see the Bamber Boys," as the group was commonly called locally.

She did, and struck up a working agreement which brought the trio before the public on several radio stations, and as representatives of New Jersey at the National Folk Festival, held in Washington on May 1, 1941.

The Pinehawkers claimed that some of the music they played was brought to the Pines by pirates who sailed up the Forked River from Barnegat Bay to hide, and that it was handed down through the generations. Bill Britton, who died in July, 1977, even had a "family dance" which the Brittons claimed as their very own.

The name Pinehawkers is an old-time reference to residents of the Barrens. The group stayed together until

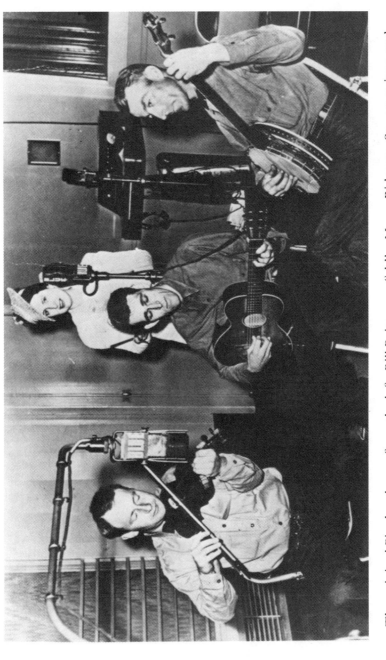

The original Pinehawkers—from the left: Bill Britton on fiddle; Merce Ridgway, Sr., on guitar; and Walt Britton on banjo. Standing is Dorothea Dix Lawrence, the radio personality who did so much to bring the Pinehawkers before the public. (*Photo courtesy of Merce Ridgway, Jr., who received it from the late Elmer Britton.*)

The current Pinehawkers—from the left, standing: Pete Curry, Glenn Borden, Merce Ridgway, Jr. Kneeling: Lenore Franzen and Arlene Ridgway. (*Photo courtesy of Merce Ridgway, Jr.*)

World War II, when two of the three were called for
military service. Merce, Sr., was excused because of a lame
leg brought on by a buckshot accident in his early childhood.

The trio came together again after the war but eventually broke up because "everyone was tired," according to
Merce, Jr.

The traditions of the original Pinehawkers are being
carried on today by the new group headed by Merce
Ridgway, Jr. Young Merce, like his father, is a bayman
playing gigs on the side. He is assisted in the latter by Pete
Curry, banjo; Glenn Borden, fiddle; Arlene, Merce's wife,
mandolin and vocals; and Lenore Franzen, fiddle, mandolin and vocals. The group has performed at the New
Jersey Folk Festival in New Brunswick and various other
Eastern folk events.

My first acquaintance with the Pineconers, who are
currently carrying on the tradition of Pines music as well
as old-fashioned band dance tunes, was at the December
Folk Festival at Whitesbog, a sixty-seven acre holding of
the Conservation and Environmental Studies Center in
Lebanon State Forest, which for the past two years has
sponsored an outstanding folk weekend.

The place was named for Elizabeth White, the early
twentieth century New Jersey horticulturist who first cultivated blueberries in the Barrens. Most of the year
Whitesbog is a quiet little collection of wooden buildings,
but it is jumping when the festival is underway. How the
people—hundreds of them—even find the place is amazing,
since it is well off the beaten track on an old dirt road that
threatens to mire your car at the slightest hint of wetness.

Dress is casual. Beards and large brimmed farm hats are
also a part of the picture. It was in this atmosphere that
I met Janice Sherwood, Gladys Eayre and Sam Hunt
for the first time. They were trudging up the road trying

to avoid deep pools of water, carrying their instruments with them.

The Pineconers are specialists in what they call "old-time music," rather than any set style. Janice does the vocals and plays banjo, Gladys also does vocals and plays guitar while Sam Hunt, a real Piney from way back, plays banjo and does "comments," while Joe Albert, now in his eighties, plays a mean "gut bucket," or washtub bass. A Toms River player, Kurt Kievel, Joe King from Waretown, and Janice's daughter, Katie, occasionally appear with the band.

Janice, who is business manager and song collector for the group, sums up its activities. "We want to do old-time songs, but most of all we want to get people out and doing music themselves, like they did in the old days before radio, TV and the movies.

"At the hall (Albert Hall) some come back several times to listen and then show up one night with instruments of their own. They are always asked to join in. We ain't too particular. We just want everyone to have a good time and bring back the social spirit that once was."

As the trio and I made our way to a small building with a sign "practice hall," they unpacked and sat down to tune up and chat.

Banjo player Sam Hunt, who seems to delight in his role as a character, not only picks a hot banjo but delights in story telling. When not playing, Sam makes Barnegat Sneakboxes, small boats native to the Barnegat region. The yard of his cluttered place at Waretown always has three or four boats in the process of being put together.

Sam is a South Jersey original, a man whose spirit is alive to the rhythms and riches of the Pines, the sea, the back bay and cedar swamps. He figures he has been making Sneakboxes for about thirty years and playing the banjo a lot longer. Sam names among his acquaintances the famed

The Pineconers at Waretown—left to right: Janice Sherwood, Gladys Eayre, Joe Albert on gut-bucket, and Sam Hunt.

folk singer Pete Seeger, whom he met years ago, and who asked him to join him in a New York show. Sam just never got around to it.

Born in Glendora, Camden County, in 1912, he said his father was supposed to have been part Cherokee Indian and was sixty-seven years of age when Sam was born.

Hunt worked for the sheriff's department and country road force in Ocean County for about twenty-three years before retiring to build boats, pick the banjo "and do some dancing." He claims he can still out-dance almost anyone in the Pines.

On his story-telling side, his favorite yarn is about the time in 1947 when he went fishing off Long Beach Island and in less than six hours landed more than 2,350 pounds of fish—an all-time record.

Gladys came from a musical family, but she had to teach herself to play. As a teenager she was one of a group of ten young people who got together at Waretown. She later sang in a gospel quartet, but discovered she could get money for singing secular songs in the Ocean County area inns. Two of her favorites at the time were Eno's, which stood on Lacey Road in Forked River, and the Greyhouse on Route 9, also in Forked River. She has collected melodies wherever she has gone and estimates she has close to 250 tunes in her collection.

Janice and Gladys are cousins. It was a Saturday night session that brought the two women together as performers. Janice is a niece of the late fiddler Uncle Bill Britton. It was not until 1966 that she began to play the banjo. She borrowed one from her uncle. When this needed repairs whe was recommended to Sam Hunt, who introduced her to "the crowd" at the Homeplace. She has been a Pineconer ever since.

When I asked Gladys what were the first songs the group

played, she answered in her straight-forward way, "Can't rightly remember. We just played 'em, we didn't name 'em."

However, she did recall "Mountain Hornpipe," "Great Cove Time," and "Moonshine Ballad" as among favorites. Some of today's crowd-pleasers are "I Like Mountain Music," "Bill Bailey," "Y'all Come," "Green, Green Grass of Home" and the "Wabash Cannonball," for which they get constant requests. In deference to modern tastes the Pineconers have added "Country Roads."

Originals of the area which have become part of the repertoire are, "I'm Going Back This Very Day," and "Home in the Pines," by Bill Britton; "Homeplace," by Joe King; "Pines of Bamber," by Kurt Kievel; and "Come on Down to Waretown," by Pete Curry.

A few other dedicated Pinelands musicians and folk people are Bruce Sturtevant, singer, musician and humorist; the Lost Weekend Swamp Stormers, from Hunterdon County; Pay Parsons, Phil Anthony, Pete Curry and Jim Jabonski.

One who should be listed with the crowd is Jimmy Albertson of Mauricetown, whose specialty is telling Pineland tales by the use of puppets. He currently heads the New Jersey Folklore Society.

With these kind of dedicated people, Pines music and folk stories live on.

Honkers and Squawkers

The early Pineys living near the seashore marshes learned the art of duck decoy carving from the Lenape Indians. They refined the craft, perfected it, and handed it down to each succeeding generation up to the present time, when pine belt decoy carvers, proud of their work, are considered the best in the nation.

Decoy carving can be considered a pine belt primitive art. Not only is a decoy identifiable by individual artistic touches, but by the regional name it is given. Maine decoys, for instance, are known as "floaters," while Massachusetts hunters call them simply "decoys." But no respectable New Jersey Pinelands duckman would refer to them as anything but "stools." As their function is to attract live ducks into the range of the hunter's gun, the term is appropriate.

Continuing the duck decoy carving tradition that started with his great-grandfather or perhaps even before that, is Gary Giberson of Port Republic, a current member of the colorful Giberson clan. His forebears fanned out over the greater part of the South Jersey woodlands as far back as 1680, when the patriarch of the family arrived from Finland via England to cut himself a 3,200 acre plot of land in the Pines, in the vicinity of what is now Port Republic. This land is still in the family.

The first Gibersons were hunters, trappers and fishermen. Most of them still are. Gary, who lives on the family tract of woodlands, secures most of the wood for his carving from his own land.

Back in the first days of duck decoy making, each hunter carved his own. From these carvers emerged such top artists of the Pines as Gene Henderson and Jack Updike, along the Mullica River, and Harry Van-Nuckson Shrouds, the "Tuckerton master" down nearer the shore. Rowler Horner was also tops in the art. Updike, according to

Gary—who was working away on a new creation when we attempted a chat amid flying chips—knew every turn of the twisting Mullica and every tree stump sticking out of shallow water. The Tuckerton carver always claimed that anyone could use a knife but "you have to know ducks, what they looked like in their most natural positions, and what kind of stools would attract other ducks. Ducks are wise. They can spot a phony fast. That is why the successful carver must know every inch of the bird, feather positions, and what coloring to use at the time of year planned for use of the stool."

In addition to being a duck carver Updike was also a carpenter, painter and tall tale specialist. One of his favorites was about the Continental soldiers who would take a day off from hunting the British to hunt and cook ducks right along the Mullica. It seems a likely enough yarn to most Pine Barrens hunters.

Gary is one of those industrious Pines characters who does not believe in wasting valuable daylight time, and he continued whittling away as we talked, surrounded by handmade tools of his own invention, a couple of Sneakboxes (the duck hunting craft popular in the South Jersey marshes especially around Barnegat, Tuckerton and Waretown) and a half dozen stools in various stages of completion.

Giberson says that if nobody interrupts him he can turn out a wooden duck every twenty-four hours, completed and painted. At times he has done this to keep abreast of orders from city hunters who have not the time or skill to carve their own. Gary estimates that he makes about ten decoys a week when he's working at it. Today a dozen hand-carved decoys sell for $250. Giberson's own work sells from $25 to a high of $300 each, a far cry from 1945 when he was selling for $36 a dozen.

Gary Giberson, member of the famed Pine Barrens Giberson clan, at work in his Port Republic workshop.

He likes to say that his ducks have individuality. There are some Canvasbacks, Old Squaws, Hooded Mergansers and Mallards. Most popular in the South Jersey marshes are Canada Geese, Brant, Blue Bills, Broad Bills and Black Ducks; the latter are the hunter's favorites. "Mallards," says Gary, "are the least likely stools to attract duck flocks that happen to be passing."

And there is another bit of specialized vocabulary you need to know if you want to talk duck with these Pines duckmen, and that is the difference between a honker and a squawker. A honker, Gary explains, is a goose, and a squawker is a duck!

This proud Piney, who can change into a backwoods dialect at the bat of an eye, has been carving ducks since he was twelve years old. He learned his craft in traditional manner, taught by his father and grandfather. On this particular afternoon he was putting feathers on a stool, using a sharp expert tap of his blade which produces natural looking plumage. "Look out for flying chips!" he warned me. Asked it they were a hazard to him, he replied in a Piney twang, "Nope, I trains 'em to go the other way."

Gary recalls having heard the old folk discussing duck carving of the Indians, and he told me that the Lenape practiced a form of taxidermy. They would take the outer skins of ducks and place them around bunches of meadow grass or hay to make them resemble live fowl.

The Piney wood carver seemed distressed that his art is fading, save for a handful who still prefer the old methods. "Ninety percent of wood decoys today are mechanically made," he observed. "Relatively few are hand carved. Many on the commercial market are made of styrofoam and cork. Somehow they work. Maybe the ducks are just dumb."

Gary says that many of the hand tools in his collection came from former carvers who have gone to machines.

"When you learn to use your hands and head, you become a craftsman. When you learn to use your hands, head and heart, you are an artist." Some samples of Gary Giberson's art.

"You need to be a good craftsman to use old tools," he said, "as each is designed for an individual operation." He still spurns the bandsaw for larger cuts, preferring to use instead a big bow saw and a few other tools he has invented. Gary likes to sum up his carving philosophy this way: "When you learn to use your hands and head, you become a craftsman. When you learn to use your hands, head and heart, you are an artist."

He has fond hopes of some day establishing a duck decoy museum in the Pines to preserve a dying art. In this he is being encouraged by Fred Noyes, formerly of the Historic Towne of Smithville, who has also envisioned such a place. The Noyes collection, an extensive one, will be the nucleus of the undertaking. Giberson meanwhile is traveling the backwoods trails of the Pines searching out works of early masters.

Gary estimates he has carved about 3,500 decoys in his lifetime. Many of these were sold in "rigs." This is a term used for a group of wooden decoys. There are usually a dozen to a rig, although there could be more. He has appeared at various folk festivals in the area, including stints at Smithville's Old Town and Wheaton Village, Millville. Gary is presently teaching a group of high school students the old crafts of the Pines.

His workshop is located in a small wooden building in Port Republic which once housed the Amanda Blake country general store. It is on a street that today looks much as it did in post-Revolutionary times, due to the unceasing efforts of Port Republic residents to keep the old traditions alive.

Language of the Pine Barrens

Many a visitor to the South Jersey Pine Barrens has come away completely frustrated after attempting to hold a conversation with an old-timer of the area. The usual complaint is, "They don't speak English down there." The puzzled outsiders are wrong. The natives do indeed speak English, but unless you are acquainted with a number of local terms conversing may be difficult.

The area was settled by English and Irish Quakers, the Dutch, Swedes, Germans, Scots, Russians and Poles, each adding their own special expressions to the language. When a Swede could not pronounce a German word and a Scot could not twist his burr around a Polish one, there was a compromise which created something akin to a combination of Pennsylvania Dutch, Ramapo Mountain, and Appalachian hillbilly, plus the salty vernacular of the New England fisherman.

Many of these word combinations orginated in the Pinelands; others were brought in from time to time, as newcomers arrived. Here is a sampling of a few of the most picturesque words and terms you are liable to run across.

Apple Palsy—A strictly Pines expression meaning the results of too much applejack.

Antmires—Ants

A Point—A fork in the road.

Beant going—I am not going.

Barnegat Sneakbox—A certain type of small fishing or hunting rowboat favored by Barnegat area sportsmen. Mostly homemade.

Basket sloop—Mays Landing area expression for a sailing

vessel coming up the Great Egg Harbor river to the landing for provisions.

Bellywax—Molasses candy

Bellywhistle—A homemade soft drink of molasses or honey, vinegar, nutmeg and water.

Boarding in the kitchen—Taking meals at the mansion house; a Martha Furnace phrase.

Boughten—Referring to article other than a gift; an article not handmade. Also, store-boughten.

Breaker—Apprentice boy whose job it was to break glass objects from a blower's staff in glass furnace during hand blown glass era. A job requiring a certain amount of skill.

Calico-bush—Laurel

Can't rightly see—Cannot understand.

Chasing the cat—Practice of shoemakers and other tradesmen, going from farm to farm in makeshift wagons to sell their goods and take orders.

Clam Towner—Resident of Tuckerton.

Clammer—Anyone making a living of digging clams in bay waters.

Clandestine retreat—Quitting a job without notice.

Coaling—Making charcoal

Coal-bugs—Charcoal burners

Come for fire—When neighbor would borrow hot coals to start fire in his own fireplace.

Cotton Dollies—Localism of Mays Landing. Women who worked in its cotton mill.

Cripple—Term used by eighteenth century South Jersey map makers, meaning a swamp or bog.

Crowhawk—A large clam

Dish of tea—A cup of tea

Door Yard—Area surrounding the back door of a house.

Drowned land—The marsh adjacent to a stream or river.

Eel grass—Certain type of meadow grass. Gathering was once big industry, especially in Ocean County.

Fingerboard—A Pines expression for where roads meet; more verbal than written.

Flye—Low meadow (borrowed from the Dutch).

Foreign man—Confined to Jersey shore language, meaning anyone from inland settlements. In the 1800s a resident of Burlington City was a foreign man to a resident of Absecon.

Frog—A railroad crossover. Early reference to a "frog war" in Cape May County had nothing to do with meadow creatures but concerned a railroad dispute.

Gollykeeper—South Jersey cuss word of 1800s. No translation.

Grass hats—Straw hats, strictly seashore slang.

Happy as a clam at high tide—Barnegat baymen expression of 1800s.

Happy as a skunk in a whirlwind—Strictly Pinelands expression for extreme happiness.

Hero behind the stove—One who talks more bravely than he acts.

Herrin' run—Spring migration of herring in the Great and Little Egg Harbor Rivers.

Highball—Stage coach term. A metal ball on a chain in front of a stage stop. (One still hangs at Smithville.) When the ball was hoisted to the top of the post the driver knew there was no need to stop; a lowered ball meant passengers awaiting.

Hog Berries—Wild huckleberries

Hog iron—One name for Jersey swamp bog iron.

Hollow ware—Pots and pans

Hurtleberry—Eighteenth century for wild hurtleberry or huckleberry, the cultivated blueberry of today.

I bent going—I am going.

Jagged fingernail—A stepmother; not complimentary.

Jersey Lightnin'—Applejack whiskey made by the Pineys.

Ketchy—Fisherman's language refering to changeable weather.

May Pinkin'—Gathering arbutus in the woods.

Menders—Another form of meadows.

Muster—Childbirth, as in "she's expecting a muster."

Nooin—Taking time off for lunch.

Old Eph—A blue heron

Pretty middling smart—Feeling good.

Pineballing—Picking pine cones and selling to wholesale

florist firms. This was a favorite bit of activity for Pineys after the cranberry picking season.

Piney—One who lives in the Pines. Often misused to denote backwardness. Pineys were and are more industrious than many writers give them credit for being. Today's Pineys are proud of this designation.

Raising ore—Digging bog ore from Pineland streams.

Rat-tanning—Spanking

Roundabout—A short jacket

Stewed Quaker—Mulled cider

Sawyer—Worker in a sawmill.

Sciencing a road—A Pinelands expression for paving.

Scoopin'—Harvesting cranberries in bog area. Before the mechanical scooper came into being this was done with a wooden scoop.

Sea ketched—Food from the sea.

School took up—School started

Shacklin—A lazy person

Skyscraper—One who has a high opinion of himself.

Sled day—In most woodland areas, December 1.

Slaken person—Lazy person

Snew—Gloucester county, past tense of snow.

Stump jumpers—Backwoodsmen

Surf clam aristocracy—Person who thinks too much of himself.

The ready—Expression for cash money.

Taint do it—It isn't so.

Turkles—Turtles

Ten fingers—Oysterman's expression for a thief.

Waspers—Wasps

Weighty Man—A man with intelligence, a bookkeeper, school teacher, land owner.

Whoopee road—A place in the Pines where moonshine is made or bought.

With hides on—Potatoes cooked with skins on.

Woodjin—A guide to the Pine regions.

The Bird Doctors

Cinderella is a sassy-faced but friendly raccoon who was born in the chimney of a small Pine Barrens home. The cottage's elderly lady occupant was terrified at the sight of the small ball of fur that one night came crashing down into her fireplace. Believing that she was being attacked by some Pine Barrens demon, she quickly lit a fire to force the creature back up the chimney from which it had come. The little thing did not make it, and by the time the woman realized what had happened, the infant raccoon had been badly burned, had lost all its claws, and broken a leg.

Luckily someone notified Mark and Martha Pokras, lovingly referred to in the area as the "bird doctors of the Pines." They rescued the little unwanted visitor, carefully mended its broken bones, and, after sitting up a few nights to soothe its crying because of its hurts and the loss of its mother, nursed the little raccoon to where it took a new interest in life.

That was a year ago. Today, the beautifully marked baby is queen of the M*A*S*H*-like collection of cages, coops, and miniature wading pools (old tubs) that stretch over the Pokrases' land. They have cleared fifteen acres far back in the Pines in the vicinity of Oceanville and the Brigantine Wildlife Preserve.

Amateurs in bird and animal handling when they began their unique venture, the Pokrases were aided along the way by two county veterinarians who gave freely of their time and skills. Today, Mark and Martha consider themselves much better qualified to follow their avocation than when they first started. Their work is recognized by state and county game officials. Both are marine biology instructors at Stockton State College in Pomona.

The "Pine doctors" treat most of their patients with a view toward returning them to their natural habitat. Unfortunately, this will not happen with Cinderella, since she will never be able to fend for herself in the wilds without claws. Someday—and both Mark and Martha are very vague about this—the little raccoon may wind up well cared for in a nature center. Meanwhile, she is definitely queen of all she surveys, and definitely spoiled.

Then there is Whoo, the owl which was brought to the Pokras rehabilitation center after the bird lost a leg in a steel leg-trap set by hunters, a practice the Pines doctors deplore as barbaric.

Whoo was unable to catch food or otherwise take care of himself, and would have starved to death had he not been rescued. He arrived at the center about a year before this writing. Today he has learned to make his one good claw do the work of two. With continued improvement he will some day be taken to the Brigantine Wildlife Refuge and returned to his natural surroundings.

Whoo considers himself a very important part of the household, with a large enclosure all his own. He keeps a pair of sharp eyes on all who venture near.

A short time ago repairs to a church belfry in Steelman-ville, on the edge of the Pines, was delayed considerably by the presence of five young barn owls who also ended up at the Pokrases' center until they were ready to tackle the wilds.

Herbert Higbee and son Dan, both of Steelmanville, were preparing to repair the roof and steeple of the Palestine Bible Protestant Church. When they put their heads across the opening of the belfry they were greeted by a series of frightening hisses.

"We thought they were snakes," said the elder Higbee, "but on closer inspection we found these young owls." They called Mark Pokras. Crawling into the small space inside the steeple, heavily gloved, Mark removed the baby owls. He mused that if the proverbial church mouse

Mark Pokras prepares to release a barn owl.

survived at all at Steelmanville, it did so against great odds, since an adult owl cosumes as many as forty mice a night. Farmers of the area have encouraged owls to nest in their barns for this reason.

Church pastor the Reverend Mr. Trump said he had delayed repairs as long as possible because of "my owls."

"We enjoyed watching them fly in and out of the steeple. It was a beautiful sight on a summer evening."

The church owls rested at the Pokrases' place until it was deemed they could take care of themselves. One evening there was a royal fly-away.

Then there is Chico, a hawk which has been a six year guest slowly recovering the use of its wings. A couple of ducks occupy an enclosure with its own private swimming pool (tub). They are two of a much larger group of wild ducks rescued from an oil spill, and will shortly be released along the migratory trail. The oil is finally gone from their delicate feathers.

A duck itself has no way of removing the heavy oil and will die if it does not receive human aid. Even with the modern techniques developed to combat this contemporary problem, only about twenty-five percent of the victims of a spill will recover.

In the six years Mark and Martha have been conducting their unique venture, they estimate that they have housed more than 800 birds of different species. During Hurricane Bella they treated as many as forty to fifty sick and injured birds per day, working around the clock. During migratory periods there have been as many as 200 birds housed in the chicken wire and plywood flight cages, victims of injury of one kind or another. Recently the Pines bird doctors gave every effort they could muster to save the life of a rare Peregrine falcon after it had been shot. The bird recovered and is now part of a breeding program at

Chico, the Red-tailed Hawk, whose wing was destroyed by gunshot. It will never fly in the wilds again.

Cornell University, where a study is underway to save the fast disappearing species.

The whole Pokras operation is strictly non-profit. The Pine Woods couple spend the greater part of their earnings as teachers on their wild friends "with no regret. We are doing what we want to do," said Mark. "Maybe some people would think we were nuts of a kind, but when we watch one of our patients take wing and fly high in the sky it makes everything worthwhile. This is the life we like. We love the Pines and the peace and would not give it up."

Mark and Martha dream of the day when they might be able to build a more efficient bird hospital, with the help of a possible grant, but until then they continue to make house calls to pick up wounded birds or small animals, to treat them with what skill they have, plus lots of love, and to rejoice when they return to their own wild lives.

Here's Pineland Mud in Your Eye!

When you see a Major League baseball umpire reach down at the start of a game and rub mud on the baseball about to be thrown to the pitcher, he is not using just any old mud but "black cold cream," dug from the bed of a certain stream leading into the Pine Barrens somewhere in the vicinity of Willingboro, N.J.

This particular mud, which has the qualities needed to make baseballs less slippery and pitchers much happier, was discovered back in 1938 by Major League baseball player Russell "Lena" Blackbourne, a Cincinnati Reds infielder, later a Chicago White Sox manager, after he had tried mud and silt from many other localities, including the Ohio valley streams.

Rubbing mud on a baseball is now as traditional to the game as an umpire taking a small broom and dusting off home plate. In fact, a can of Blackbourne's mud is now housed in the National Baseball Hall of Fame in Cooperstown, N.Y. And thereby hangs a little known tale of old South Jersey.

"Lena," so named because of his lean stature, resided near what is now Willingboro. He discovered the special qualities of the mud in a nearby stream bed and took a sample to the diamond. His team's pitchers found that it gave them a firmer grip on the ball. It was also noted that the mud never discolored the ball cover.

Word spread to the other Major League teams and soon the Cincinnati outfielder found he was swamped by demands for his New Jersey mud not only from clubs in his own league, but the other as well. It is now ritual for an umpire to rub about five dozen baseballs with the mud before the start of every big league game, including the World Series.

Blackbourne, keeping his mud-digging location a closely

guarded secret, was supplying all the majors up until 1968. At that time he became ill and turned over the business— and by then it was a successful one—to a lifelong friend, John Haas, who continued to dig and can the product in coffee-size tins.

After he reached eighty-four years, Haas found trips to the creek beds more than he could handle and transferred the unique undertaking to his daughter, now Mrs. Betty Haas Bintliff, also of Willingboro, who has since carried on the business. Mrs. Bintliff, who has nearly enough offspring to start her own baseball team, is confident that when she quits her active role in the mud business there will be young Bintliffs to carry on.

The product is now called the Lena Blackbourne Rubbing Mud. The location of the place in which it is found is a carefully guarded family secret. Mrs. Bintliff contends that the business has its side benefits—she gets to meet all the big stars of baseball and, being a fan of long standing, this is worth the effort of sometimes making personal deliveries.

Mrs. Bintliff is the one who coined the phrase "black cold cream."

Bibliography

Manuscripts, Personal Letters, Notes and Family Records

Atsion Furnace accounts, Burlington County Historical
Society.
Baseball Hall of Fame, Cooperstown, NY, data from files.
McMahon Collection, Atlantic City.
Brumbaugh, G. Edwin. "Historical Aspects of the Wharton
Tract." McMahon Collection, Atlantic City.
————. Letters concerning company stores, especially Batsto
stores, written to the author. McMahon Collection, Atlantic
City.
Butler, Frank. Unpublished letters and manuscripts. McMahon
Collection, Atlantic City.
Carter, Annie. Notes on Pine Barrens flora. McMahon
Collection, Atlantic City.
Fritz, James Mason. Mason family letters and documents.
McMahon Collection, Atlantic City.
Gillespie, Angus. "Folk and Hillbilly Music in the Pines,"
Proceedings, First Annual Pine Barrens Research
Conference, New Brunswick, 1978. McMahon Collection,
Atlantic City.
———— and Tom Ayres. "Folklore in the Pine Barrens; a Study
of the Pinelands Cultural Society of Waretown." McMahon
Collection, Atlantic City.
Green, Charles F. Unpublished manuscripts. McMahon
Collection, Atlantic City.
Halpert, Herbert Norman. *Folk Tales and Legends from the New
Jersey Pines; A Collection and a Study.* Unpublished doctoral
dissertation, Indiana University, 1947. Special Jersey Pines
collections, Stockton State College, Pomona.
Martha Furnace account books, Camden County Historical
Society.
Pugh, Delia. Letters. McMahon Collection, Atlantic City.
Ridgway, Merce, Jr. A personal history of his father, founder of
the Pinehawkers. McMahon Collection, Atlantic City.
Toughill, Frank. Letters and special notes about his feature
stories in Phiiadelphia newspapers. McMahon Collection,
Atlantic City.

Historical Society Files

New Jersey Historical Society, Newark
Port Republic Historical Society, Port Republic
Camden County Historical Society, Camden
Gloucester County Historical Society, Woodbury
Ocean County Historical Society, Toms River
Burlington County Historical Society, Burlington City
Hammonton Historical Society, Hammonton
Cape May County Historical Society, Cape May Court House

Newspapers

The Press, Atlantic City, including *Historic Towns* series,
    1958–1959; *Heritage Edition,* April 12, 1964
Courier Post, Camden, including *Centennial Edition,* May 19, 1964
Hammonton News, Hammonton, including *Centennial Edition,*
    May 19, 1966
Salem Sunbeam, Salem, 1976
Batsto Citizens Gazette, Batsto, 1970–1978
Burlington County Herald, Burlington, Dec. 12, 1949

Library Collections

Atlantic City Library, Atlantic City, Heston collection
Ocean County Library, Toms River, archives
Stockton State College Library, Pomona, special Pinelands
    collection
Newark Public Library, Newark, Archives and History Bureau
New Jersey State Library, Trenton, special collections
Rutgers University Library, special N.J. collections

Printed Sources

Bisbee, Dr. Henry W. *Sign Posts.* Burlington City: privately
    printed, 1971.
Blackman, Leah. *History of Little Egg Harbor Township.*
    Tuckerton: originally part of an 1880 West Jersey
    Surveyors & Association report; reissued by Great John
    Mathis Foundation, Trenton Printing Co., 1963.

Boyer, Charles W. *Early Forges and Furnaces of New Jersey.*
   Philadelphia: University of Pennsylvania Press, 1931.
   ————. *Old Inns and Taverns of West Jersey.* Camden: Camden
   County Historical Society, 1962.
Buell, Murray F. and Beryl Robichaud. *Vegetation of New Jersey.*
   New Brunswick: Rutgers University Press, 1973.
Burgess, Paul C. *A Colonial Scrapbook.* Brigantine: privately
   printed, 1971.
Coad, Oral. "Jersey Gothic," *Proceedings of N.J. Historical Society.*
   Newark: April 1966.
Federal Writers Project. *New Jersey, A Guide to its Present and Past.*
   Trenton: Hastings House, 1939.
Green, Charles F. *A Place of Olden Days.* Egg Harbor City:
   privately printed, no date.
Heston, Alfred M. *South Jersey, a History.* New York: Lewis
   Historical Publishing Co., 1924.
McCloy, James F. and Ray Miller, Jr.. *The Jersey Devil.*
   Wallingford, PA: Middle Atlantic Press, 1976.
McPhee, John. *The Pine Barrens.* New York: Farrar, Strauss and
   Giroux, 1967.
McMahon, William. *Town of Hammonton.* Hammonton:
   Hammonton Historical Society, 1966.
   ————. *South Jersey Towns in History and Legend.* New
   Brunswick: Rutgers University Press, 1973.
   ————. *Historic Towne of Smithville.* Egg Harbor City: Laureate
   Press, Vol. I, 1967, Vol. II, 1975.
Miller, Pauline. *Early History of Toms River.* Toms River: privately
   printed, 1967.
Peterson, Charles J. *Kate Aylesford.* Philadelphia: T. B. Peterson,
   1855.
Van Hoesen, Walter H. *Early Taverns and Stagecoach Days in New
   Jersey.* Rutherford: Fairleigh Dickinson University Press,
   1976.
Wacker, Peter. *Land and People.* New Brunswick: Rutgers
   University Press, 1975.
Wise, Harry B. *History of Applejack.* New Brunswick: New Jersey
   Agricultural Society, 1954.

Index